Rai Bahadur Ram Saran Das of Lahore

Nilima Lambah, known as Nina amongst her friends, graduated from Lady Shri Ram College, Delhi University and taught for a brief period before marrying Satinder Lambah, an Indian Foreign Service officer. As president of the Indian Women's Association in Pakistan, Germany and Russia, she was actively involved with charitable organizations in the host countries and in India. In Russia she was elected president of the International Women's Club, Moscow. Extensive travels with her husband brought her in contact with well-known personalities from diverse fields in different countries. She was invited for a private lunch by Mrs. Putin, wife of the Russian President, on the completion of her husband's tenure as Ambassador to Russia. Russian Protocol officers described it as perhaps the only instance of a First Lady of the Soviet Union/Russia hosting a meal for a departing Ambassador's wife. On a subsequent visit to India she made a request for a meeting with the author. Prime Minister Vajpayee then invited the author and her husband for a private dinner which he hosted for Mr. Putin. Nilima Lambah is fond of reading, art and music. She has two children and lives in Delhi.

Comments for Nilima Lambah's book,
A Life across Three Continents: Recollections of a Diplomat's Wife:

"I extend my compliments to Smt. Nilima Lambah for having authored this valuable book."

—Shri Pranab Muherjee, President of India

"The memoir is a rare social history of India's diplomatic service"

—*The Indian Express,* 7/12/08

"A candid cavalcade of interesting episodes, anecdotes and fascinating experience culled from a life lived in a host of countries... Written simply these recollections have something for people of all ages and from all walks of life."

—*The Hindu,* 2/11/08

"...the Pakistan chapters are most engrossing, unsurprisingly... The account of the Zia years is an evocative one."

—*The Hindu,* 5/4/09

"There are rib-tickling anecdotes...the two chapters [on Pakistan make] a particularly fascinating study with close encounters with Benazir Bhutto and Nawaz Shariff as well as Bhuttos' nemesis and Nawaz's patron the shrewd and scheming dictator Gen Zia-ul-Haq."

—The Indian Foreign Affairs Journal, Jan-March 2009

"Enables the reader to envisage all the places where the Lambahs stayed and gain a vivid pictures of the cultural, social and geo-political aspect of each individual country as well as the personal experiences tasted by them in these countries...the anecdotes included in the book add to the reader's enjoyment of it..."

—*The Dawn,* Pakistan, 8/2/09

Rai Bahadur Ram Saran Das of Lahore

The Grandfather I Did Not Know

~

NILIMA LAMBAH

RUPA

Published by
Rupa Publications India Pvt. Ltd 2020
7/16, Ansari Road, Daryaganj
New Delhi 110002

Sales Centres:
Allahabad Bengaluru Chennai
Hyderabad Jaipur Kathmandu
Kolkata Mumbai

ISBN: 978-93-90356-29-4

Third impression 2021

10 9 8 7 6 5 4 3

Printed at Saurabh Printers Pvt. Ltd, Noida

Contents

I)	History of Lahore	1
II)	R.B. Mela Ram and the Ancestral History of the Family	32
III)	R.B. Ram Saran Das	42
IV)	Manifold Activities and Reminceses of Ram Saran Das	51
V)	Lahore and Politics During the Time of Ram Saran Das	74
VI)	The Punjab Legislative Council	83
VII)	R.B. Ram Saran Das as the Longest Serving Member of the Council of State (1920-1945)	88
VIII)	Death of R.B. Ram Saran Das and Media Reports on His Death and Funeral Procession	138
IX)	Partition 1947	150
X)	My Paternal Grandmother and Aftermath of Partition	160

ANNEXURES

1)	Article on Ram Saran Das reproduced from N.B. Sen's book, 'Eminent Hindus of Punjab' published in 1943, two years before the death of Ram Saran Das	166
2)	Two articles on Ram Saran Das and his father Mela Ram by Professor Tahir Kamran published in the Pakistan newspaper "The News" on February 19 and 26, 2017, written 72 years after the death of R.B. Ram Saran Das.	174

3) Family Tree of R. B. Ram Saran Das 183
4) Arbitration Award distributing the properties of Ram Saran Das amongst his five sons. 188

Acknowledgements 206

R.B. Ram Saran Das of Lahore (1876-1945)

Mela Ram (1832-1890) Father of R.B. Ram Saran Das and founder of the family business

Mela Ram Building.
Courtesy: Fakir Syed Aijazuddin's book Lahore Recollected

CHAPTER 1

HISTORY OF LAHORE

A brief insight into the evolution of Lahore would help in understanding the contribution made by my paternal great grandfather R.B. Mela Ram and grandfather, R.B. Ram Saran Das to this historic city.

Lahore, situated on the banks of the River Ravi in Punjab, aptly known as the land of five rivers, was destined to play a significant role in the history of the subcontinent of India. According to legends, Lahore, initially known as Lavapuri, was founded around the first century by Prince Lava, son of the ruler of Ayodhya, Lord Ram. The amalgamation of the name Loh, by which Prince Lava was also known, together with the Sanskrit word 'awar' or fort, evolved into the city being eventually known as Lahore. There still exists a vacant temple in Lahore Fort (now in Pakistan) dedicated to Lava.

An ancient document, Hudud-i-Alam (The Regions of the World), written anonymously in 982 was published as late as 1927 in Lahore, following its translation into English by Minoesky. It describes the Lahore of that era as a 'shehr' or town inhabited by infidels or non-Muslims with "impressive temples, large markets and huge orchards". Reference is also made to "two major markets where dwellings exist" and "the mud walls that enclose these two dwellings to make it one". The original document is kept in the British Museum.

Over the centuries various travellers made mention of

Lahore in their writings. Faxian, a Chinese, in 414-399 BC, the Egyptian astronomer Ptolemy in his famed Geographia in the 2nd century and Hiuen Tsang, a Chinese, in the 7th century.

The first Muslim invasion took place in the late 7th century.

For the next four centuries, Lahore was captured, plundered and burnt by invading hordes. However, by the 11th century it evolved into the regional capital of the Shahi Kingdom. Later in the 12-13 century it became the capital of the Ghund State under the Delhi Sultanates.

The mercurial ascent of the Moghuls in the 16th century, resulting in three hundred years of dynastic rule, was a period of construction of palaces, mosques, pavilions and gardens.

In 1611, William Finch, an agent of the East India Company, described Lahore as one of the greatest cities of the East.

In 1641, Fray Sebastion Mannque, a Spanish monk, wrote, "The city of Lahore is beautifully situated commanding the agreeable view on one side of the river with crystal waters which descend from the mountains of Kashmir... Lahore is ornamented with fine palaces and gardens, also tanks and fountains...".

The 19th century witnessed the establishment of the Sikh empire in 1799 by Maharaja Ranjit Singh, who ruled for forty years.

A British officer, Charles T. Metcalfe described the Lahore of 1809 as a "melancholy picture of fallen splendour. Here the lofty dwellings, masjids, which, fifty years ago, raised their tops to the sky and were the pride of a busy and active population, are now crumbling to dust". After touring the place he added, "... that on going over these ruins, I saw not a human being, all was silence, solitude and gloom."

Two centuries of warfare, starvation and disease had

reduced this metropolis into large fields of rubble and debris.

As the Maharaja's army proved no match against the superior European artillery, British colonial rule was officially established in 1849.

THE BRITISH RULE

The British came to India initially as traders. The East India Company was founded on the last day of the year 1600, following the defeat of the Spanish Armada in 1588. Queen Elizabeth I granted 'a Charter of Rights and exclusive trading to 'the Governor and Company of Merchants of London Trading into the East Indies'

In 1615, Sir Thomas Roe, the first British envoy to India, met with the Moghul Emperor Jahangir to seek protection for English trading factories or warehouses in Surat. Subsequently, the British set up trading posts along the coastal regions of the sub-continent of India, exploiting differences between local rulers to their advantage. Experiencing unbridled success in trade, their stance significantly changed. In 1757, following the defeat of Bengal in the famous Battle of Plassey and drunk with ambition and greed, they resolutely set on a course of conquest of the sub-continent.

In 1831, Lieutenant Alexander Burnes arrived in Lahore with a cargo of thoroughbred Arabian horses. These were gifts from Britain's King George IV for Maharaja Ranjit Singh, symbolizing a gesture of friendship and co-operation. It was in reference to this that Burnes wrote, "We made our public entrance into the imperial city of Lahore which once rivalled Delhi." According to Burnes the ancient capital extended five miles east to west with an average breadth of three miles.

The death of Maharaja Ranjit Singh in 1839, followed by

the unstable state of affairs for the next decade provided the British the opportunity to annex Lahore to their expanding empire. Colonial rule was thus established in 1849, in the granary of India, their 'jewel in the crown.'

Traditionally the economic base of Lahore was mainly dependent on agriculture. The foremost occupation of the people was growing vegetables and crops with a parallel emphasis on dairy produce. People led simple lives and livelihood was drawn on lines based according to the tribe, caste or birdari affiliated with it. This division was instrumental in controlling the spectrum of behaviour of an individual and family. The village artisans and domestics were, at time of harvest, paid in grain for services rendered. This system was called Sep, and some artisans received Sep, once or twice a year.

Lahore, at this juncture of history, served as one of the important destinations for traders travelling long distances along the ancient Silk Route. This Middle Eastern and Central Caravan route historically represented the final border between West, Central and South Asia. Trade served as the crucial strand that bound and intertwined diverse countries along this long and arduous journey, resulting in a barter of grains, nuts, spices, textiles, raw material and the intermingling of culture and languages. Serais, set up for the convenience of traders traversing the extensive Silk Route, were positioned within a day's journey to protect both merchants and cargo from the dangers of the night. Each serai provided meals, resting places to sleep and bathe and the facility to sell their goods at a bazaar. Merchants were able to meet, exchange experiences and gather useful information. A serai of vital significance for the Sikhs was referred to as Lahore Sharif. For the Muslims, it represented links to the Mughal and Sufi past—the city of Data A Hujwi—the Sufi who spread Islam to this corner of South Asia.

Serais were constructed outside the gates of Lahore. The scene at a serai was one of intense activity. The noise reached a crescendo when traders boisterously vied to settle accounts amidst the hustle and bustle of bales and bundles being loaded and unloaded along with the grunting of beasts of burden. To give reprieve to exhausted, thirsty travellers and animals, refreshing cool water was drawn from wells. Food and resting places were simultaneously made available. Old grooms were paid off, and the new ones recruited for the next leg of the journey. The atmosphere of interaction generated both momentum and vibrancy. R.B. Mela Ram, my great grandfather, too built a serai outside the Bhatti Gate.

The Lahore of 1837, during the time of my great grandfather, was self-contained, and referred to as 'Un-droone- Shehr' or inner city. It could not have been more aptly described as the city was confined within the high boundary walls constructed during the reign of Mughal Emperor Akbar in the mid-16th century. It had thirteen gates and each gate was befittingly named after rulers, saints, ancient landmarks or a city in India towards which it faced. The names of the gates were Akbari Gate, Bhatti Gate, Delhi Gate, Kashmiri Gate, Lahori Gate, Masti Gate, Mochi Gate, Mori Gate, Roshnai Gate, Shahalmi Gate, Shairanwala Gate, Taxali Gate and Yakki Gate. These were securely closed at night and constantly guarded to thwart any threat from potential enemies.

The entire structure of the walled city was interestingly based on Havelis, Mohallahs, Koochas, Katras and Galis representing centuries-old associations with Afghans, Tughlaks, Lodhis, Mughals and more recently, the Sikhs. It contained the grand fort, palaces, tombs, mosques, residences, buildings, narrow alleyways and open spaces. The city was arranged in a neat pattern. On each side of the bazaars were the mohallas, which in turn, were divided by a broad street. Within the mohallas were the koochas or lanes and katras.

The havelis, beautiful large residences belonging to the nobility and affluent class, represented a masterpiece of architecture and heritage. These were lofty brick buildings with innumerable rooms, verandahs, balconies, huge kitchens and a basement to keep people cool during the hot summer. A fountain normally occupied a prime location in the centre of a large and open courtyard used primarily for ceremonies and functions.

The Mohallas were residential areas where the rich and the poor lived side by side in houses of varying sizes and quality. Some were three to four storeys high. The Muslims, Sikhs and Hindus lived in separate mohallas, but worked and interacted with each other on a daily basis.

The gallis or alleyways were a world unto themselves. Densely populated and lined on both sides with brick houses, they served the dual purpose of both a commercial and residential complex. Street vendors roamed the gallis, making known their ware to prospective customers in loud singsong voices. Occupants, particularly those living on the upper storeys, had a novel way of purchasing goods and settling accounts. Pragmatically, a basket tied to a rope was lowered and filled with the necessary requirements, then raised to the level of the purchaser, who, after off-loading the goods, put the money into the basket before lowering it again. Women folk were thus able to shop without stepping out of their homes, in accordance with the custom of that time. Each narrow lane or a galli offered its own service facilities in the form of water carriers, washer men, cobblers, tailors and doctors or hakims, proving beneficial and profitable for all. The bazaars were colourful and throbbed with life adding to the vibrant ambience of the 'undroone-shehr'.

For the benefit of those with limited space, provisions were made for wedding halls or 'Jang Ghars'. The groom traditionally arrived quietly seated on a horse to the venue of marriage—a total contrast to the deafening music and vigorous Bhangra dancing of today.

Life was uncomplicated and people followed a set routine. The simultaneous wailing of sirens from the North-West Railway Loco shop and Makaner Lal's factory announced the dawn of a new day. Spiritual calls emanating from surrounding mosques and the simultaneous tinkling of myriad bells from temples marked the commencement of the day's worship. For the Sikhs too, Lahore held great significance, as it was the land of the Gurus, Nanak and Arjun and more recently the capital of Maharaja Ranjit Singh's Sikh Empire. Thereafter, many visited Minto Park for an early morning walk, yoga or exercise, before proceeding for work.

With the men gone to attend to their work, women immersed themselves in household tasks. With domestic chores completed, they met neighbouring ladies on the roof top. Here they knitted, embroidered or gossiped across partitioned walls while the carefree laughter and shouts of children filled the air. During winter they basked in the glory of the sun.

The residents of the walled city were referred to as 'Lahoris'. Belief in good and bad omens was a common trait all over India and more so in Lahore. Meeting a scavenger en route to work was considered lucky, whereas a cat crossing your path was unlucky. Twitching of the right eye for a woman and the left for men was considered a warning. The falling of a lizard on the head was auspicious. Sweeping the floor at night was inauspicious. At the onset of a journey or anything important, to sneeze was considered a bad omen. To ward off the effects of the 'evil eye' lemon and chilli totems were commonly used.

Ironically, the belief that sighting a Brahmin brought bad luck made one believe that Brahmins were not held in the same high esteem in Lahore as they were in many other parts of the country. Paradoxically, in each house in Lahore, a Brahmin priest played a multi-purpose role. Whether it was to recite prayers, make astrological predictions, conduct a wedding, perform the rituals at the birth of a child or on any other auspicious occasion, he was undoubtedly indispensable.

The walled city had its share of negatives too. Smoking opium, drinking country made liquor and gambling were rampant vices. A lack of underground drainage, together with sordid heaps of waste and garbage in the narrow over crowded gallis, made it environmentally unhealthy. Due to the offensive smell emanating from the drains, the British referred to it as a 'city of decay and gutters.'

Following the annexation of Lahore in 1849 by the British, Sir John Lawrence described the area surrounding the walled city as 'an uninhabited rough terrain made up of ruins, kilns of several layers of brick, with the soil being burnt by saltpeter dust. Here and there some Moghul tombs and other monuments were still standing.'

The insalubrious congestion of the walled city together with the desire to be segregated from the local population led eventually to the creation of a new city by the British on the 'uninhabited rough terrain,' and Lahore experienced an evolutionary change both in structure and way of life.

The British, in a bid to win over the locals, initially lowered previously imposed taxes which was a much appreciated move. But shortly thereafter, with a metamorphosis in British policy, sweeping changes took place in agrarian and administrative sectors. These coupled with the imposition of rigid laws wrought havoc and life became difficult. Taxes originally paid in kind, were now to be paid in money, forcing people to borrow from money lenders, particularly after a bad harvest. Over taxation made many abandon their traditional occupation of agriculture. The liability of revenue collection lay on the shoulders of the landlord or zamindar. In villages, the responsibility of paying the revenue was on those who owned the village.

Increase in taxation affected all—the artisans, the labour class, farmers and traders. None were spared. Taxes on export of agricultural products and import of British industrial goods promoted only British interests and adversely affected the locals by increasing their indebtedness and poverty. Severe and coercive methods used to collect taxes led to the ruin of many.

For administrative purposes, the British-controlled areas were divided into several divisions and districts with Lahore district being one of the twenty seven districts of Punjab. As their primary goal was maintenance of law and order and collection of revenue, policies were accordingly formulated and implemented. They manipulatively gained acceptance of various groups by favouring them with rewards and awards. The local chiefs who were heads of castes, tribes or biradaris, were the beneficiaries of their largesse, thereby enabling them to rule over vast areas and the huge population with a small administrative set up. Caste and biradari became the institutional keystones of Punjab society.

An event of great significance in the life of the common man was the introduction of a printing press. The 'Lahore

Chronicle', the first English newspaper, made its debut in 1849. This was followed by the birth of the first Urdu paper in 1850. Following the Mutiny of 1857, the press was 'gagged.' With the government controlling the printing press, circulation of news harmful to their interests was withheld. In later years too, with growing Indian nationalism, freedom of press was curtailed.

According to Narendra Singh of Sarila, "The great Sepoy Mutiny of 1857 triggered a revolt by Indian Princes whose territories the British had grabbed up during their conquest of India".

The British rule, a mixture of policies of coercion and conciliation led eventually to a rebellion. The rumour that the fat from the cow (sacred to Hindus) and pig (Haram for Muslims) were used to cover cartridges which had to be removed by mouth by the native soldiers, was the last straw that ignited a revolt within the army. There were widespread protests in 1857, which was , in reality, India's first war for independence. The British chose to call it a Mutiny and crushed it mercilessly.

Post 1857, a discernible change in the attitude of the British towards the Indians became more evident. From the beginning they exploited and treated them with disdain, but now following the insurgence, suspicion and hatred widely prevailed. Intimidating and vicious steps of oppression were taken against those who had fought in the revolution. Many were hanged, several languished in jail and thousands were left to live in humiliating conditions. Lands belonging to the Jagirdars were drastically reduced or simply taken away and the Sikh Khalsa Army was disbanded to prevent any further uprising.

With a large number of troops stationed near Lahore, severe punishments were meted to those suspected of disturbing peace with seditious activities. Another drastic measure taken was the demolition of seven gates to de-fortify the city. Today, of the original thirteen gates, only six stand—Delhi gate, Bhatti Gate, Kashmiri Gate, Lohari Gate, Roshanai Gate, and Shiranwala Gate.

The British, to expedite access to various areas of the vast territory under their control, constructed roadways. The creation of a network of roads across extensive stretches of land not only made the task of exploiting their colony easier, but also helped improve connectivity within the country. By 1850 the Grand Trunk Road from Lahore to Peshawar was made.

Simultaneously, roads were also made to facilitate communication within the city. The Mall Road made in 1851 by Lieutenant Col. Napier, to directly connect Anarkali to Mian Mir was constructed at the cost of ₹10, 428.

Amidst all these happenings, there was another major development. A Government of India Act, passed in 1858 by the Parliament in U.K, called for liquidation of the East India Company with transference of its functions to the British Crown with immediate effect.

With this transition, realisation that compromises had to be made in order to rule over a vast country like India, dawned on the British Government. Due to acute shortage of personnel, some areas were left under the control of princely rulers, indirectly dependent on the British Government. The princely states known as Native States, were technically not part of British India, as neither had they been conquered nor annexed by the British, but were, however, subject to subsidiary alliances.

With the British Government taking control of Lahore, emphasis was laid on development. The first evolution, in the eastern part beyond the 'inner city', was the construction of a military cantonment covering 1,312 square metres. Barracks, training fields and offices were set up for officers.

In 1861, the British commenced the construction of a modern Lahore, half a mile to the north-west of the old city that came to be known as the Civil Lines. With both residential and commercial housing constructed for their comfort, the British imposed their own way of living on the natives whose language, culture, climate and concept of life was vastly different from their own. This exposure had its own impact and reverberations over a period of time.

While coming from Mian Mir in 1875, it was reported that there was nothing to be seen after crossing the canal but barren plains on both sides of the road. The Maharaja of Patiala's palatial bungalow was the sole exception. The empty stretch between Anarkali and Mian Mir was filled up later, as reported in a newspaper, "The Railways, an entirely new and separate Department with its large staff and bringing with it an enormous following of workmen and their families, filled up another great gap in the new site".

By 1875 the British population exceeded 1,700. This led to the growth of commodity trading and the opening of retail and grocery shops to meet their requirements.

The Gol Bagh on the Lower Mall became the hub of activity in Lahore. As the police band played here twice a week, it was given a new name—The Bandstand Gardens. People thronged to this venue which served as a social rendezvous for the gentry, to exchange views, gossip and enjoy the ambience created by scintillating music. The common mode of transport was by horse- drawn carriages.

More English newspapers came into being. In 1872 'The Civil and Military Gazette' was followed a decade later by

'The Tribune' in 1881. Although Urdu papers were already in existence, a Punjabi newspaper, 'The Khaba Akhbar Lahore,' began publication in 1887. Collectively these helped to create a new awareness. Lahore soon became the hub for the printing industry. By 1896, there were seventeen printing presses and two decades later there were seventy-five.

The most significant contribution by the British, which left an everlasting impact, was the introduction of the railways. They systematically envisioned, planned and engineered the entire process and painstakingly instructed Indian labourers how to build them. Railways enabled them not only to control and rule this huge disconnected and diverse country, but also to facilitate the transport of raw material. Wherever a resource was located, a railway line was laid to connect it to the nearest main line thus ensuring smooth transportation. Materials such as cotton, timber, coal, aluminium, iron-ore, tea, gold and precious stones were transferred to a nearby port and sent thereafter to their final destination in England. In reverse, goods from England were transported to various ports and put up for sale in Indian markets. With railway lines laid directly inland from major ports, the British were not only able to consolidate their power but were also able to economically exploit the country to their advantage.

Makeshift trains to transport material were introduced as early as 1835. By the last decade of the 19th century, food and grains were exported to faraway markets. To facilitate transport of mail, officials, labourers and soldiers to various destinations within the country, passenger trains came into being. The first passenger train to be operated was from Bombay—a fourteen coach train hauled by three steam locomotives!

However, these developments were at a cost to history. Bringing the railways to Lahore, the 'Pearl of India,' meant laying waste to a large number of mosques, palaces, gardens and monuments, as the British demolished almost every trace of Mughal and Sikh structures, to make military barracks, schools and hospitals. It was Lord Curzon, a lover of Indian archaeology, who four decades later, put an end to this rampant destruction. Nonetheless 'the British did succeed in enriching the architectural heritage of the city in a remarkably unconventional Mughal-Victorian style.' (Balbir K Punj, *On an Ancestral Trek*)

By the turn of the 20th century, an era of peace and prosperity was established. Lahore gained the reputation of being the richest and most progressive state in Northern India as it was an important commercial and industrial centre.

Industry was of two types—cottage and industrial. The cottage industry comprised of all forms of handicraft products made by carpenters, shoemakers, potters, bricklayers and metal workers. Products ranged from pottery, basket work, lacquered ware, cotton weaving, embroidery, metal work, enamel, wood engravings and shoe making. Gold and silver jewellery were made by craftsmen who reputedly flourished under the patronage of the Royal Court, the Chiefs and Sardars. Fine silks and brocades catered to the demand of the elite. The British, critical of the colour, composition and mythological themes of traditional art, including miniature paintings, only preferred landscapes, human figures and portraits. As such products were now made to suit changed demands.

Simultaneously, an industrial revolution was taking place. With Lahore's newly developed economic foundation based on manufacturing, commerce and administration, it became in the 19th century, not only the centre for repairing railway carriages and locomotives, but also the headquarters of the military garrison. Metal fabrication, moulding and lathing industries were established, thereby laying the groundwork of creating an industrial base in the city. Railway and locomotive workshops laid the foundations of an industrial base and Lahore was soon recognized as the largest centre for the engineering industry.

Cotton ginning, flour mills and numerous other factories gradually emerged in response to changing demands. In 1897 my grandfather, R.B. Ram Saran Das, set up the first spinning and weaving mill in the province. By 1911, forty three mills had come into existence. These were set up primarily for cotton ginning and pressing, grinding flour and husking rice. Cotton produce still remains one of the main industries of the city.

The construction of the Cantonment, Railways and the Bari Doab Canal together with an expanding bureaucracy saw an increase in labourers and white collar workers. With government offices, public and private banks, insurance companies, warehouses, commercial centres, all having a presence, opportunities were created for advancing the status and fortune of individuals, resulting in the emergence of a solid middle class. Several buildings and bridges were constructed by the firm belonging to my grandfather. As the city grew, so did the economy and soon enough, 32 English, and over 100 vernacular periodicals added to nation-wide comprehension of current happenings and affairs.

The citizens of Lahore belonged mainly to three religions—the Muslims, the Hindus and the Sikhs. Muslims were primarily rural dwellers, Hindus lived mainly in the city and as the Sikhs were engaged in land cultivation and military services, they lived in both the rural and urban areas. Muslims constituted 51% of the population. The Pathans, Gujjars and Kashmiris dominated the Muslim population. The famine in Kashmir in 1878-79, resulted in many Kashmiris migrating to

Lahore. Pathans came only during winter to find jobs. Hindus composed 35%, Sikhs 12%, Christians, Buddhists etc, 1% of the population. The population which was 125,413 in 1868, rose steadily by 1921 to 202,964.

Christian missionaries arrived with the sole purpose of converting the locals to Christianity. Threatened by this onslaught and to protect the interests of their own religions against the zest and zeal of Christianity, a new culture of priests and clergy emerged amongst the Hindus, Sikhs and Muslims. They countered with motivated determination, the efforts of the Christians who were trying to establish supremacy. Lahore became the hub of religious activity leading to the collective rise of the three dominant religious organisations—1) the Hindu Arya Samaj, Hindu Mahasabha and RSS, 2) the Islamist Ahrar and Khakisan and 3) the Sikh Singh Sabha and Akali Dal. All religions echoed diverse aspirations. To purify the dubious practices and superstitions within each, and to keep pace with the changing times, some reform movements were instituted.

But social reform movements seeking to raise status of women, the fight against child marriage and removal of the practice of 'untouchability' always met an unrelenting wall.

British influence gradually became more evident with the establishment of the first English school- Forman, in 1849. The system of education had a major impact on the lives of people and educational institutions, as students from all communities studied together. Schools such as Aitchison School and Dyal Singh School, soon became renowned. English medium schools for girls, Victoria Girls School and Queen Mary's School were equally popular, where apart from academics, emphasis was laid on learning household skills, playing musical instruments, tennis and dancing. The Ganga

Ram High School was primarily for Hindu girls. The Anjuman-i-Himayat-i-Islam launched schools in Lahore in 1884 for Muslim girls that taught Urdu, the teachings of the Koran, needlework and other domestic skills. Enrolment fluctuated as conservative Muslim families preferred to educate their girls at home. It was not until Jinnah's famous speech in Lahore in 1940, encouraging education among girls, stating that if "political consciousness is awakened amongst our women, remember, your children will not have much to worry about", that Muslims started taking a more progressive stance where women were concerned.

Universities and colleges were subsequently established for higher and specialised education. A number of successful ICS officers were products of the Government College and the Formans Christian College. King Edward's Medical College produced many doctors; and the Punjab Engineering College and the Law College several successful professionals.

The well established Kinnaird College for women, set up in 1913, became renowned in South Asia. Initially the students were Christians, but soon Hindus and Sikhs followed and later Muslims from elite families. Due to an increasing demand, Queen Marys College and later, Lahore College for Women in 1922 were opened. The Muslim women observed strict 'purdah' and though the Hindu women did not observe 'purdah' they always covered their heads with a dupatta.

A major development was the advance in the field of medicine. Lahore was reputed for offering an array of medical services—allopaths, hakims, vaids, naturopaths, faith healers, homeopaths and ayurveds. But now medical colleges provided the city with dedicated doctors, resulting in surgeons, physicians and specialists making a debut. With hospitals fitted with the latest equipment and treatment vastly improved, patients from neighbouring places too came to find a cure for their illnesses. Professional women doctors were a new entry in the medical field.

Education played a significant role in altering the mindset of Indians. Initially faced with a dilemma, the Indians were torn between adjusting to the new colonial milieu on one hand and keeping a grip on inherited traditions on the other. There was reluctance to leave ancestral moorings, yet, as ideas of modernity gradually percolated through, and with rapid developments taking place, they were lured into expectations of a brighter future. With transformed circumstances and the need of the hour, several students enrolled in these institutions. Many Punjabi noblemen pragmatically made arrangements for their children to be taught English privately before admission to English medium schools, thereby elevating them to the status of the new elite. Hindus and Sikhs took more readily to western education than Muslims and thus the latter missed out on the initial career opportunities offered.

Over the years, educational institutions succeeded in churning out students endowed with rare qualities of perception and analytical reasoning. The students gained confidence, commanded respect, and the acquired knowledge helped keep them abreast of the rapid changes and make adjustments accordingly. Their progress encouraged many to join, leading eventually to a social and intellectual awakening.

Thus a new middle class emerged, consisting of professionals—lawyers, doctors, teachers, traders who played an instrumental role in the life of the city. As a result, the Lahore society gradually began to manifest a new social structure and etiquette.

Keeping pace with social changes, the women of Lahore soon gained the reputation of being trendsetters in fashion.

The traditional Ghagri (a skirt and blouse) was replaced by lahangas, salwar suits and the graceful sari. By 1930 the custom of early marriages gradually declined. Parents of marriageable daughters pragmatically preferred men with a secure job and a regular financial income. With a metamorphosis in concepts, educated young men too wanted an educated wife who could play a supportive role in their life. As a result, schools and ladies' colleges registered a significant increase in numbers. There were several instances of young married successful men leaving their simple and uneducated wives to marry educated girls with a better social standing.

The metamorphosis in perspective of city life, provided women several opportunities to venture out of their homes, opening up manifold channels of interest.

But despite changes in outlook, girls were never put at par with boys. Inheritance was the sole right only of men. Girls at the time of marriage were given a limited dowry, in comparison to the practices of today. For a mother-in-law, a dowry was not as important as the daughter in law's ability to beget a son.

The traditional mode of dress for Indian men drew a subtle line of demarcation between different classes. The common man wore a lungi which was an unstitched material wrapped around the waist that hung up to the ankles. A loose shirt was worn on top and during winter, a plain woollen shawl draped around the shoulders was the sole addition.

The affluent Hindus dressed in long graceful coats or achkans with churidar pyjamas while the Muslims wore long elegant coats known as sherwanis with salwars. The summer outfits were made of silk and winter ones of English woollen worsted fabrics. The rank of an individual could be deciphered depending on the quality of material worn. Added accessories by the more fashionable included gold buttons, matching waistcoats, mufflers and gold chains with pocket watches.

The head dress or pagri, considered a symbol of honour, varied in style according to rank and class. There was a marked difference between a pagri or turban worn by a Hindu, Muslim or Sikh with each being indicative of the personality, rank and status of the wearer. Made of fine muslin, many matched the colour of their pagri with their clothes. The most striking pagri, according to author Pran Neville, was sported by the Tiwana family.

By early 1930 British influence became significantly apparent with the change of the apparel of men. The pagri lost out to fedoras and caps, the long sherwanis and achkans to short coats, and salwars and churidars gave way to trousers held up by braces and belts. Peshawari sandals were replaced by fashionable leather shoes and collared shirts and ties became the new entrants resulting in a complete revolution in the form of dress. By the end of the 1930's, shorts, shirts and solar hats were the established uniform for school boys.

The saying that clothes make a man may well be true. Members of the Legislative Assembly (MLAs) were elegantly dressed, wore impressive turbans and lived in great style in their private mansions, or, if they were out station visitors for a session, in hotels. Members of the Congress wore Gandhi caps. Whether they were in the ruling party or in the opposition the MLAs were held in great esteem, on account of their honesty, integrity and dedication. The concept of black money and corruption did not exist and was unknown at that time. It is widely believed this commenced during World War II.

Under the British, a 360 degree turn was made in the form of travel. Traditionally, heavy loads were hauled by bullock carts and lighter goods carried by donkeys—a slow and cumbersome process. Public transport was restricted, either by bullock cart or by a single horse driven light carriage called a tonga. Parked at vantage points, the tonga drivers, primarily Muslims, would announce destination halts to potential customers. For conservative women in purdah, a cloth screen set up in the carriage ensured privacy. Within the confines of the walled city with its winding narrow alleys, the palki or palanquin carried by four men, remained the most pragmatic mode of transport.

The launch of bicycles took Lahore by storm. The Raleigh brand, fitted with a dynamo light and a number lock, available for ₹60, was most in demand. Following closely on its heels, costing between ₹40 to ₹50 were the brands by Hercules and Phillips. By 1935, the innovative Japanese entrepreneurs introduced a cycle costing only ₹19, resulting in it being accessible to a far greater number of people.

Till the mid 30's the common mode of transport by the elite were luxury coaches drawn by horses called buggies or Victorias. A total revolution took place with the introduction of motor cars. (My grandfather was the first to import a car in Lahore.) Soon, both British and American imported cars made a grand entrance on the streets, and it was not long before cars rubbed shoulders with bicycles and Victoria carriages on the roads of the city. The realisation that motor cars were not only speedier, but were also easier to maintain than horses, made them even more in demand. The popular cars of that era were the Morris (priced at ₹1800), the Fiat (₹1800), the Baby Austin (₹2,500), the Opel (₹2,200) and the Ford (a little less than ₹5,000). Petrol was available for one Rupee and four annas per gallon.

Initially cars belonged to a select few—the Governor of Punjab, the Commissioner of Police, the Chief Revenue

Officer, senior British personnel and some others of official standing, but over the years, these gradually increased in number. Motorcycles were used mainly by the police.

Buses, as a means of public transport, replacing the tonga, commenced service in 1945. Initially, they transported people from the railway station to all the main gates of the city, but soon their radius widened. This was followed by the introduction of an Inter-city bus service to various destinations such as Srinagar and Rawalpindi which left at a fixed time. Being cheaper than rail travel, this soon became the more preferable form of transport.

A change also took place in the form of entertainment. Earlier it was limited to fairs, religious processions and festivals where all communities participated together in full fervour, irrespective of cast, creed or religion. At fairs, a variety of street food whetted appetites, while skilled magicians, jugglers, acrobats, singers, dancers, snake charmers, monkey men and puppeteers enthralled audiences. Stalls were set up with goods for sale and everyone returned happy and tired after a full day's outing.

Festivals too provided an opportunity for people to mingle in an atmosphere of merriment regardless of religion. The popular festivals celebrated with great enthusiasm were Lohri, Basant, Holi, Baisakhi, Eid, Dushera, Diwali and Gurpurav.

Another big draw was the circus. Hugely popular, people thronged to see the well trained animals and talented artists whenever it was in town.

The introduction of cinema added a new dimension in the field of entertainment. By 1947, Lahore was firmly established as the second largest film centre. With the onset of films originated the idea of advertisements. A quick succession of picture slides projected on the cinema screen, if only for a second, extolled the virtues of various products. Thus a novel way of raising revenue was established.

With appreciation of music in their blood, people flocked to hear reputed singers, the most popular being K.L. Saigal, Nur Jahan, Malika Pukhraj and Tarranum. Baithaks in the walled city trained young musicians in classical music. Other famous artists were Amrita Shergil, (daughter of a Sikh father and Hungarian mother) who died very young and B.C. Sanyal, a renowned sculptor. Hailing from Gujranwala but brought up in Lahore, Amrita Pritam gained the reputation of being the queen of Punjabi literature. Literary giants like Faiz Ahmed Faiz and Allama Muhammad Iqbal, who were intellectuals and men of letters, met in tea houses in Anarkali and the Mall to hold discussions.

The cultural season was heralded by the onset of winter and people converged to the city to enjoy the variety offered. Music, qawwalis, concerts, theatres, dance performances, libraries and museums, attracted diverse segments of society, enhancing Lahore's stature as the cultural capital. While the British stayed at hotels, the locals stayed with friends and relatives.

Sports too played a vital role in the lives of people. Wrestling, tennis, hockey, cricket and badminton were favourite outdoor sports. The popular indoor board games were chess, snakes and ladders, ludo and carrom. Kite flying was very popular, and it took on new heights during the festival of Basant, which heralded the coming of spring. Lahoris dressed in hues of yellow flocked to enjoy this festival. Prime time was spent on the rooftops and as their kites soared in the air, a pleasurable feeling of power and glory was apparent when an opponent's kite was felled. Both, the young and the old, exhibited their skill in this field with great exuberance. During Basant, the specialised kite makers, who lived in Mochi gate and Bhatti gate, were kept busy as the demand for kites accelerated sharply.

On both our postings to Pakistan (1978-82 and a decade later from 1992-95) I found Basant was celebrated with far more fervour in Lahore than in Delhi. However, in recent years, celebrating this Hindu festival has come under criticism by a section in Pakistan. Ironically, contradicting this very stance, a newspaper report had stated that Pakistan was considering celebrating the Hindu festival of Holi that marked the coming of spring, in all the kaleidoscopic hues of nature's bounty! But with a rise in fundamentalism, it seems unlikely.

The game of cricket, introduced by the British, reputedly was played for the first time in Lahore in 1848, in the open fields north of the Fort. Horse racing was another event organized by the British which soon gathered momentum. The first racing club, established in 1924, came to be known as The Lahore Race Club.

The highlights of tourist attractions in Lahore were the remnants of the architectural monuments and gardens constructed by the Mughals. Making water colour drawings of these was a favourite pastime of British memsahibs. Author Faqir Aijazuddin in his book 'Sketches from a Howdah' displayed the watercolour of the Shalimar Gardens made in 1860 by Lady Charlotte Canning, wife of Viceroy Charles Canning. He also brought to note her letters written to Queen Victoria together with vivid observations in her journal of the scenery while travelling within India. Interestingly, she wrote about her visit to 'Khurtarpore,' presently called Kartarpur where she was shown some of the earliest copies of the Sikh Holy Book, the Granth Sahib. Guru Nanak, founder of the Sikh religion, lived in Kartarpur for 18 years where he assembled a

Sikh community. He died there on September 22, 1539. Almost four centuries later, Maharaja Bhupinder Singh of Patiala is said to have donated ₹1,35,608, for the making of Gurdwara Darbar Sahib on the site where Guru Nanak died. With the partition of the country, Kartapur became a part of Pakistan. In 2018, this very city made headlines when Pakistan offered to open a corridor to enable Sikh pilgrims to visit the place where Guru Nanak died. This was opened with great fanfare in November, 2019.

With all these happenings Lahore gradually rose in importance, replacing Delhi as the centre of literary activities. It became the vortex of intellectual, cultural and political life where a constellation of artists, poets, journalists and writers met. Though Persian was the language of the court during the Sikh period, it was officially replaced in the 19th century, by Urdu, but in the Persian script.

Over time, Lahore gained the reputation of being a multi-faceted city. The pivot of international markets, it housed the administrative quarters of Punjab and became the centre of educational institutions.

The class divide between the natives and the British became sharper with the arrival of memsahibs. Clubs, parties, and an indolent lifestyle became the norm. Clubs offered members facilities of enjoying tennis, music, good dining, ballroom dancing and a bar serving alcohol. The cost of a bottle of Scotch whisky was ₹11. Few British mixed with the locals but some Indians were permitted to join the Club.

The Anglo-Indians came into existence in the 18th and 19th century when the British came to India unaccompanied by their women. By 1930 the Anglo-Indians were a sizable community that considered themselves superior and a cut above the Indians. Trusted by the British they were gainfully employed in the railways, posts and telegraphs. Though 99% of them had never been to England they referred to it as home. Their biggest assets were the command of the English language and willingness to take on indispensable tasks. Despite this the British had limited social contact with them.

The surging economy manifested itself in the opening of new shopping markets. The mile long Anarkali Bazaar, stretching from Lohari Gate to Nila Gumbad, was ranked the queen of bazaars and was named after Nadira Begum. Renowned for her beauty and known in history as Anarkali or the 'Pomegranate Blossom,' she met with a tragic end. Emperor Akbar displeased at the growing relationship between Anarkali and his son, Jahangir, had her walled and bricked alive. Later his son, Emperor Jahangir built a beautiful mausoleum over the grave of his beloved.

Anarkali Bazaar, a shoppers' paradise, was bustling with activity in the early 20th century, flourishing after World War 1 and renowned by the late 1920s. A visit to Anarkali was a stimulating experience. An array of products lured customers—flowers, fruits, toys, stationery, shawls, durries, bedspreads, steel trunks, shoes, Peshawari chappals, crockery, utensils, watches, clocks, books, perfumes, medicines, jewellery and gramophones. A variety of textiles were available—imported chiffons and georgettes at ₹1 per yard, Double Horse Bosky at 12 annas per yard, English woollen suiting between ₹7-10 a yard and English cotton voile at 6 annas per yard. Exquisite embroidery on satins and velvet too were on display. The bazaar vibrated with life. Adding to the bustle was the discordant cries of hawkers, vendors and fortune tellers, selling their ware on busy streets. It boasted of restaurants, bars and hotels and students spent hours in the evenings at various tea stalls, engrossed in lively discussions.

Ladies arrived in tongas and carriages, but due to the prevalence of the 'purdah' system were reluctant to enter shops. However, without much ado, the enterprising shopkeepers resolved the problem. They carried their wares to the carriages, enabling ladies to make a selection. By the 1930's, ladies came without purdah, a step not initially approved of. Soon, with the change in outlook, a visit to Anarkali was not only considered fashionable but a must.

Several smaller bazaars catering to a specific trade were equally popular. Sara Bazaar was renowned for jewellery, Kinari Bazaar for silver and gold thread embroidery, Bazaz Hatti for cloth and materials, Kasera Bazaar for copper and steel utensils, Papadmandi for provisions and spices, Dabi Bazaar for wholesale items, Juti Bazaar for footwear and Landi Bazaar for second hand garments. The cantonment Sadar Bazaar catered to the demands of the lower ranks.

Situated in a prime location within the heart of the capital of Punjab, the upmarket Mall was undisputedly the most fashionable shopping centre of the city. By the turn of the 20th century some areas of the Upper Mall were electrified making it all the more alluring. Referred to as 'Chandi Sarak,' it was watered daily to keep it clean. A popular destination for the elite, it was lined with large and imposing European commercial buildings and shops. 'Eduljee,' the wine shop, several draper and tailor shops such as Mehras and Cheap John. Large stores like Jankidas, Devichand, Leela Ram, Glamour, Dhumi Chand and Kirpa Ram, the Regal cinema, Stifles Hotel, the Lorang Restaurant, large showrooms displaying a range of cars, a coffee shop—a favourite haunt of the students and intelligentsia, and commercial banks represented by the Lloyd Bank and the Reserve Bank of India all had a presence here.

Post the takeover by the British Crown, a statue of Queen

Victoria, covered by an exquisite marble canopy, took pride of place at Charing Cross in the middle of the Upper Mall. Here, the Punjab Legislative Assembly rubbed shoulders with Uberoi Sports, F.H. Pitman, Plaza Cinema, the Melaram Building that housed several shops and the Metro Restaurant. The Nedous Hotel, Lahore Zoo, the immaculate English style Lawrence Gardens and the imposing entrance to the Government House were situated in the same vicinity.

Though the Hindus, Muslims and Sikhs shared a common Punjabi culture, each maintained a distinct identity of their own. Lahore, despite being the home of multifarious communities with cultural, religious and social diversities, was basically a communally harmonious city with each relying for everyday livelihood and prosperity on the other. They worked together in friendship and cooperation. There were, however, occasions when riots did break out on communal lines.

The Hindus and Sikhs largely contributed to the economic activity in the city. They controlled the industrial sector, dominated retail and wholesale trades, owned several shops in the Anarkali Bazaar and the Mall, traded in gold and silver, food grains and textiles. They also worked in white collar jobs. Between them, both communities owned 80% of the property in the city. As Hindus were also money lenders, their Shylock-like attitude in all likelihood, generated resentment.

The Muslims did more manual labour working in fields and factories. Comparatively very few Muslims engaged in business. Only 20% of factories were owned by Muslims, out of 97 banking offices, 7 were run by them, of 80 insurance companies only 2 were managed by them and of the existing 56 colleges and schools they ran only 16. Mostly artisans, labourers and traders, they controlled fruit, dry fruit and vegetable markets, the milk supply, furniture, tailoring and shawl shops. They were not employed as civil servants or professionals. This changed once the government policy of job reservation came into being, resulting in their number increasing in the services.

Though the Hindus and Muslims lived in separate neighbourhoods, there were some areas where they lived together. The Muslim landed aristocracy owed its wealth and status primarily to the British government. Reputedly though the Hindus were considered frugal spenders they gave much to charities. While there were some men of means amongst the Lahore Muslims who were involved in works of charity, it was always Lahore's non-Muslim philanthropists who were in the lead in this area. The Ganga Ram Hospital, the Gulab Devi hospital and Janki Devi hospital were ample proof. The Hindus donated to charity, regardless of the religion of the beneficiaries. A hospital for the treatment of animals was also set up by them.

Evolving in their own peculiar way, the three communities found means of circumventing the structure of Orthodox Hindu, Islam and Sikh, thus creating a heterodox way of life that was based on mutual respect and affection. Hindus would shower flowers and sprinkle rose water on Muharram processions from their balconies, while Muslims would flock to the great Ramlila festival held in Minto Park. Muslims also took part in the Diwali and Dussehra celebrations. Hindus while passing a mosque would respectfully fold their hands. Orthodox Hindus did not eat food cooked by Muslims, but Muslims had no such inhibitions. This was because the Muslims ate beef while the Hindus held the cow as sacred. This divide was extended even to water which was sold as Hindu Pani and Muslim Pani. However, the same Hindus had no problem accepting fruit and gifts from Muslims. Intermarriage between the two communities was not acceptable.

Prior to the outbreak of World War II, an upgraded Lahore in infrastructure offered several job opportunities. Education and innovative inventions helped create an awareness that succeeded in dispelling age old ignorance and superstitions. Improvement in the transport system countered the isolation and parochialism of the Punjabis. Interaction between the British and Indians in multiple-fields played a significant role in laying the framework for development and progress futuristically.

By adapting favourably to the transformation taking place, Indians were able to better their lives. Men of wealth and social standing gradually moved to the newly constructed Civil Lines. At the same time, an emerging class of urban professionals, journalists and lawyers also bought bungalows in the same area.

The Civil Lines offered spacious bungalows with abundant surrounding land, a stark contrast to the over-crowded and squalid conditions within the enclosed city resulting in a more comfortable lifestyle. Food was cheap. The cost of a dozen eggs was 1 anna and 1kg of fish or meat was 4 annas. According to people the living was good.

The Hiramandi Bazaar of Lahore was also renowned. Aptly named Hira Mandi after a nobleman reputed for his love of wine, women and song, it was also referred to as the 'Diamond Market'. A pleasure seekers paradise, it came alive at night and was frequented by the rich, famous, young and poor. Renowned for its singing girls and courtesans, it was essentially considered a place of culture. During Mughal times, the girls inevitably found their way to the royal court, where they enchanted the nobility with music, dance and poetry. However, with the coming of the British, they passed through difficult times and only survived due to the patronage of the royal families and the emerging landed gentry.

By 1940, contractors, businessmen and merchants became their benefactors. A new trend developed, whereby the singing and dancing girls enlarged their clientele by visiting hotels and private homes. This exposure expanded their horizon and Hira Mandi is reputed to have produced some of the most famous singers, actresses and dancers of India.

A tribute paid to the city in the words of Bapsi Sidhwa best describes its emotional pull.

"To belong to Lahore is to be steeped in its romance, to inhale with each breath an intensity of feeling that demands expression."

CHAPTER II

R.B. MELA RAM AND THE ANCESTRAL HISTORY OF THE FAMILY

The family history of Rai Bahadur Ram Saran Das can be traced back to his great grandfather Diwan Das Mal (1747-1798). A scion of a prominent family, he was respected for his multiple talents and valour. During the rule of the Bhattis or Bhangi Missal, a sect of Jat Sikhs, he held the powerful post of Commander of the Artillery with the historical Zamzama cannon under his command. This was indicative of the prestige bestowed upon him.

The Zamzama, a large bore 80 pounder cannon made from copper and brass was 14 feet 4 1/2 inches in length with a bore aperture of 9 ½ inches and was the largest of its kind made in the sub-continent. Cast in 1757 by Shah Nazir, under the orders of Ahmed Shah Durrani, it reputedly had the longest range. Two Persian inscriptions were prominently inscribed on the cannon. (1) 'By the order of Ahmed Shah Durrani, Shah Wali Khan Wazir made this gun named Zamzama or the taker of strongholds' and—(2) 'A destroyer even of the stronghold of heaven.'

The Zamzama is believed to have played a significant role in 1761 during the third Battle of Panipat. Subsequently its possession came to be regarded as an emblem of sovereignty and there was a strong belief that whoever had the cannon would reign supreme. The Punjabi name for the gun was 'Bhangi di tope' and 'Bhangiawala Tope'—Cannon of the Bhangis and later 'Kims Gun'. With the capture of Lahore by Maharaja Ranjit Singh in 1799, the Zamzama cannon came under his command and likewise under the charge of the British when they took over Lahore in 1849. Currently it is on display in the Mall Road Lahore Museum in Lahore.

In 1796, at the age of 49, a son, Dhanpat Rai, was born to Diwan Das Mal. Three years later, during a fierce battle fought between the Bhangi Missal and Maharaja Ranjit Singh's army, Diwan Das Mal was tragically killed. It is believed that instructions were issued by the victorious Maharaja to eliminate the family and confiscate the properties of the deceased Diwan. As a result of this harsh directive, the young Dhanpat Rai, was secretly smuggled out of Lahore, through the darkness of night, by his maternal grandfather and taken to the town of Batala. Though showered with love and care by doting grandparents, he grew up in comparative poverty due to the changed fortunes of the family. Nonetheless, he grew into a fine man, married a girl from a respectable Khattriya family and had two sons—Lala Ram Dyal born in 1817 and fifteen years later, Lala Mela Ram in 1832. Destiny made the younger son, Mela Ram, ably take advantage of the changing situation, when power was transferred to the British. He is credited with restoring the prestige of the family to its original glory due to his hard work, diligence and far sightedness.

R.B. MELA RAM

It was said that my paternal great grandfather, Mela Ram, after having initially faced some hardships in his youth, started life as a timber merchant. He had three children, the eldest, a daughter Lakshmi, followed by two sons, Ram Saran Das and Harkishen Das. It is believed that his luck changed with the birth of his daughter, Lakshmi. A chance encounter with an artillery expert from Ranjit Singh's army, introduced him to the lucrative business of construction. Focussed determination and dedication led to his ultimate success. With his potential recognised, he was given significant contracts by the government, after which there was no turning back and his rise was swift. The Lahore Railway Station built in 1860 by three leading contractors of that time, Mian Sultan of Landa Bazaar, Mian Mohammad Bakshi of Macchi Darwaza and Lala Mela Ram, is ample proof of the esteem in which he was held. The vast expanse of land in front of the Railway Station was converted into a park and came to be known as Mela Ram Talab. Initially, it was used for parades to welcome special guests and later for parking vehicles.

Mela Ram also played an instrumental role in the laying of the Lahore-Amritsar Railroad, which commenced services in 1880. In addition he undertook the entire Amritsar-Pathankot Railway contract, which comprised the iron-work, sleepers and masonry, completing the work well before schedule. His resourcefulness and zeal ultimately paid off and he was given a special award of ₹50,000 by the Government in recognition of his outstanding work.

Appointed 'Darbari' at the age of 37 in February 1869, he was seventeen years later in 1886, at the age of 54, honoured with the title of 'Rai Bahadur'. This was a title of honour bestowed by the British on Hindus for service to the Empire. Muslims were conferred the title of Khan Bahadur.

R.B. Mela Ram's residence was a splendid haveli situated within Bhatti Gate in Lahore known as 'Lal Kothi'. The Bhatti Gate was so named because it was here that the warring

R.B. Gopal Das, eldest son of R.B. Ram Saran Das (1897–1979) with captain of KLM Fokkertri plane.
Active in Punjab politics before and after Independence.
Photo Courtesy Indire G. Biel. Obtained from the Amsterdam Archives.

Bhattis originally set up camps, following the conquest of Multan before the Mughals established their empire in South Asia. His haveli was described as 'unique in its grandeur' and Dr. Ashiq Husain Batalvi christened the surrounding area as the 'Chelsea of Lahore'. Mela Ram reputedly organised grand celebrations on the lawns of the Lal Kothi. Today that very street, close to the Anarkali Bazaar and Bhatti Gate, is named Mela Ram Road in his memory. The Mela Ram Park has, however, since been renamed the Medina Park.

Streets in Lahore were named after those who played a role in the development of the city. Interestingly, however, in an article in a Pakistani newspaper, 'The Daily Times', Mohammad Rizwan reported that "final traces of Hindu culture in Lahore

Wg. Cdr Rup Chand (1900–1984) Departing from Delhi to Kabul to take over as India's first ambassador to Afghanistan.

would be wiped out by giving Islamic names but added, "leading lights of Lahore including civil society, members and intellectuals have unanimously blasted a Lahore District Government resolution which calls for "Islamisation" of 58 Lahore streets". Perhaps this is the greatest acknowledgement and tribute for the contributions made by leading Hindus of that era.

With the rise of several structures in the Civil Lines of

Ravi Shanker (1918–1978) Took to farming in Terai area

Lahore, the Upper Mall took on a new dimension. Towards the Eastern side of the landmark statue of Queen Victoria, positioned in the middle of the Upper Mall, stood prominently, the Mela Ram Building, which housed a row of shops. Today, the WAPDA (Water and Power Development Authority) building constructed in the 1960's stands in its place. The Mela Ram Building originally measured 21 kanals, 5 Marlas and 190 sq. feet with an open site and vacant land measuring 3 Kanals

Jagdish Chander (1920–1984) Field of Insurance (father of author)

and 2 Marlas. On its right stood the Nedous Hotel, another property owned by Mela Ram, on whose site today stands the Awari Hilton Hotel on Edgerton Road, originally referred to as Racket Court Road. We were apprised by journalist and author Pran Seth, one of the few Hindus who stayed behind in Lahore after partition, that the area from the Mall Road to the PTCL Building belonged to Mela Ram. The property had been purchased by Mela Ram, towards the latter half of the nineteenth century, for the royal sum of ₹800. ₹400 was paid in cash while the balance ₹400 was paid in instalments. The

Rajeshwar Bali (1925–2020), Excelled in field of photography

Masonic Hall, Shah Din Buildings, Post and Telegraphs office and the High Court were all situated in this neighbourhood.

R.B. Mela Ram gained the reputation of being a leading businessman and was considered a great patron of the arts. Though he himself was a follower of the Sanatan Dharma, his approach to religion was liberal. He celebrated all Hindu, Muslim and Sikh festivals with great fanfare at his residence, where people of all faiths were invited. He also held musical and dance soirees at his house which were widely attended by the gentry, nobility and royalty of that period.

Author with mother on the occasion of her wedding in 1973

Despite enjoying a privileged life himself, R.B. Mela Ram did not forget the poor, and was sensitive to their needs. He built a magnificent water tank near the Lahore Railway Station and sunk several wells in different parts of the province. He also made a serai outside Bhatti gate for the benefit of traders travelling the ancient Silk Route. A hostel was constructed in the city to feed the poor and free flour was generously distributed to beggars in the city. Donations were also made to public institutions under Government control. ₹24,000 to Delhi Hospital (1864), ₹15,000 to Central Training College, Lahore, and ₹15,000 to Lady Dufferin Hospital for Women (1886).

The present Lahore zoo, the third oldest one, is on 36 acres of land donated to the city by Mela Ram in 1872. He is said to have played an instrumental role in its layout.

Towards the end of his life Mela Ram owned a large number of properties in Lahore, numerous villages and substantial land in Multan in the Montgomery District. He died on April 10, 1890, at the age of 58, leaving behind a daughter and two sons. To his credit, he instilled the spirit of philanthropy in his sons too. It was his elder son, Ram Saran Das, who was destined to follow in his father's footsteps.

CHAPTER III

RAI BAHADUR RAM SARAN DAS

My paternal grandfather, Ram Saran Das, was born on November 26, 1876 in Lahore. By then, India had already been a colony of the British for almost three decades. A year prior to his birth, the playboy Prince of Wales, son of Queen Victoria and Prince Albert of Saxe-Coburg, visited India in 1875, on what was believed to be a very successful tour. Receptions and durbars held in his honour were attended by Indian princes and other dignitaries, making it an important and significant event. The year of his birth, Thornton and Lockwood Kipling collaborated and published the first Guide Book on Lahore. Subsequently, others such as Eastwick and Walker followed suit, by publishing reference work, projecting a view of the changing landscape of 19th century Lahore. Several watercolours, drawings and other works, available from collections in the India Office Library and the Victoria and Albert Museum, have depicted a picturesque view of Lahore of the 19th century. The visual along with the historical notes provide a graphic perspective of the life of those times. The year also witnessed the setting up of the Convent of Jesus and Mary school for girls in Lahore, which over time became renowned for its academic standards. In 1877, the year following his birth, Queen Victoria was proclaimed Empress of India.

Due to the early demise of their mother, young Ram Saran

Das grew very close to his elder sister Lakshmi. At the time of his father's death, fourteen year old Ram Saran Das was a student in Central Model School, Lahore. Later he joined the Government College, Lahore, where he studied Science, Sanskrit and History. However, with the untimely death of his uncle and left with no alternative but to discontinue his studies, he was unable to graduate with a degree. His teachers, sorry to see him leave, described him as an industrious, intelligent student with deep interest in a variety of subjects.

As the eldest male member of the family, the burden and responsibility of managing his father's vast estates, contracts and zamindari fell on his young shoulders. Not one to be bogged down by the weight of unexpected circumstances, he soon proved his worth. Devoting time and energy, it did not take him long to learn the trade and develop an insight into the family business.

A visionary, he innovatively started the first spinning and weaving Mill in the province at the age of twenty one by using the resources he inherited to good use. The Mill was formally inaugurated in 1897 by Sir Dennis Fitzpatric, the then Lieutenant Governor of Punjab. More than a thousand people were employed in the mill.

Ram Saran Das was a workaholic and took personal interest in the functioning of the mill. He worked in diverse departments to familiarise himself with the intricacies involved in running this enterprise. Because of his hands on participation in multiple-tasks—that of a Dispatcher, Correspondence Clerk and Accountant, he developed a good understanding of the operation. Active association and a quick comprehension helped him to gain the practical experience required of a Mechanical and Civil Engineer. Very soon, he was regarded as an engineer of repute, which is why the book ‘Coeval Galaxy of Sir Ganga Ram’, describes him as “an engineer as well as a tycoon of industry and banking.

Entrance to the mill was through two main gates with each prominently displaying a huge bill board, with an Urdu couplet. (The first, “M.A. ho nor baaf (weaver) aur B.A. Lohar ho, phir dekhlay mulk ki kaisi bahaar ho”; and the second, “Mulk mein hirfat sey gar ma kisi ko aar ho, har ik graduate yahan aa kar dastkar ho”.) The purpose was to attract and encourage the educated young men to become industrial workers.

A decade later, the British took a giant step in improving infrastructure by introducing electricity as another landmark. Lala Harkrishan Lal launched Lahore’s first electricity supply plant on McLeod Road in February, 1912. Ram Saran Das, taking advantage of this development, provided electricity to two of his properties situated within the same vicinity—the Mela Ram Textile Mills and the Crown cinema hall. In addition, he also had the great sufi shrine of Data Durbar, located nearby, electrified. Having electricity soon became a status symbol. Though the tariff for electricity was quite low, many could not afford it. So the usage of the more economical lamps and lanterns continued.

The introduction of electricity was an event in itself as is apparent from a Pakistani TV programme decades later. According to Akmal Aleemi, “When I was comparing in Lahore a show “Ham Log” , I asked the elderly guest from Kucha Chabuk Swaran if he remembered the coming of electricity to the city. He said he did. “The night Gohar Jan Kalkatewali sang in the courtyard of the Mela Ram Mills, the first electric bulb was lighted and it surprised everyone present”.

Over the years the Mela Ram Textile Mill developed in strides. Soon the mill had its own ginning, spinning, weaving, bleaching as well as dying mechanism. The average output of cloth during the pre-war years was about ₹400,000. "The annual value of the sales of the mill during the 1st World War, due to heavy demand, was about ₹7,200,000—two and a half times more than the pre-war level." (Ilyas Chattha)

With the passage of time and introduction of more modern inventions the potential of the mill expanded. By the end of the 2nd World War "in 1946, the mill was equipped with 16,670 spindles, 150 looms and a ginning factory that was fitted with 48 ginning machines. By 1945-46, the total value of the mill was estimated at ₹900,000." (Ilyas Chattha). Workers were employed regardless of religion. Half the workers at the mill were Muslims. The best denim used for tents was reputedly produced here.

In 1978, on the first diplomatic assignment of my husband Satinder Lambah to Pakistan, Sardar Shaukat Hyat, son of Sir Sikander Hyat, (prime minister of undivided Punjab), showed us towels from the Mela Ram Mills, which were amazingly, still being used by them, thirty years later! During this period, on a visit to Lahore, we were invited for lunch by an old family associate, an ICS officer, G Moinuddin, father in law of the younger sister of erstwhile Nawab of Pataudi, Mansur Ali Khan. At lunch, he drew our attention to the elegant white Italian marble dining table, adding it was from the canteen of the mill that belonged to my grandfather. However, he explicitly clarified that he had purchased the table at an auction, (My husband was posted twice to Pakistan. 1978-82 during the Zia years and 1991-95 during the Nawaz Sharif–Benazir Bhutto years).

The mill known as Mela Ram Textile Mill was built in the vicinity of Data Durbar, the oldest Muslim shrine in South-East Asia. The shrine built in honour of the great sufi saint, Hazrat Data Ganj Baksh, houses his remains.

Lalita, daughter of R.B. Ram Saran Das with husband Shambu Lal Puri

The 11th century was a period when mystics from Central Asia were drawn to India in search of spiritual enlightenment. Syed Ali bin Usman Al Hayari, a Persian Sufi scholar hailing from Ghazni, too travelled to the Indian sub-continent. He arrived in Lahore in 1039 AD where he chose to remain until his death, 34 years later in 1072 AD. Acknowledged and renowned as a sufi saint, he had a great following and his shrine, Data Durbar, was visited by both Muslim and non-Muslim devotees.

On our first assignment to Pakistan, my mother advised me to pay my respects to Data Darbar as my grandfather had great faith in the Sufi saint. Soon after our arrival in Pakistan in 1978, accompanied by two leading lawyers of Lahore, M.A. Rahman and Ijaz Husain Batalvi, we visited the shrine. Here I was informed that it had been given its first electric connection by my grandfather, R.B. Ram Saran Das, in gratitude for a wish granted.

There are two stories in circulation as to the reason the family had faith in the shrine of Data Darbar. The first belongs to the era of my great grandfather. When Ram Saran Das was young, he fell seriously ill. Mela Ram, it was said, stood at the steps of the mausoleum and promised the saint that if his son was cured, he would bathe the shrine with milk and set up a free food centre in the name of Lahore's patron saint. When his son was cured he kept his word and became a great devotee of the saint. Subsequently, on the occasion of the annual fest of Data Darbar, Mela Ram always offered free food to the devotees and in addition, parties of qawwals performed under colourful canopies on the lawns of his Lal Kothi. Over the years this became a tradition.

The second was connected with my grandfather. The year 1918 was witness to an outbreak of an influenza epidemic throughout the sub-continent. A countless number were afflicted and died. The three elder sons of Ram Saran Das, Gopal Das, Rup Chand and Ravi Shanker, (the younger two, Jagdish Chander and Rajeshwar Bali, were yet to be born), too fell victim to this ailment. In spite of being attended to by the leading doctors of the city, Col. Amir Chand, Col. Bhola Nath and Col. Sutherland, Principal of King Edwards Medical College, (married to princess Bamba, a great granddaughter of Maharaja Ranjit Singh) there appeared little respite in their condition. What happened later, is said to be reputedly narrated in Ram Saran Das' own words.

'One night I was asleep when there was a disturbance in the room, which woke me up. I saw an elderly gentleman with a flowing white beard dressed in white. He had a stick in his one hand and a rosary in the other. He was standing by the bed of my son, Gopal Das and was intoning something. A great fear overtook me and I shouted at him asking who he was and what was he doing? The bearded man ignored me and continued to pray. He repeated this for my two other sons. Having completed his job, he turned to me and said he was my neighbour Ganj Bakhsh and could not suffer to see me so greatly worried. Therefore, he had come to pray for my sons and said that I should stop worrying. God would restore my sons to full health.'

The three sons soon recovered.

Perhaps each experience, though at different points of time, left a lasting impression on their minds. My mother told me that under the explicit orders of my grandfather, earthern lamps or diyas were lit every Thursday without fail within the premises of Data Durbar. Legend had it that if any of the watchmen in the nearby Mela Ram Mill slept inadvertently with their feet towards the shrine, they were inexplicably flung off the bed!

'The Tribune' the Chandigarh edition dated January 8, 2012 in an article, 'Lahore's crumbling gateways' by Salma Mahmud stated that the Bhatti Gate was the most splendid, adding, 'Just outside Bhatti Gate stands the mausoleum of Data Gunj Buksh, one of the greatest Sufis of the sub-continent and it is nearby in his Lal Kothi that the noted contractor Rai Bahadur Mela Ram resided, who laid the Lahore-Amritsar railroad in 1880. He was a devotee of Data Ganj Buksh and his son Rai Bahadur Ram Saran Das held musical concerts every Sunday at their havelli to which connoisseurs of all creeds were invited.'

Ambitious and hard working, Ram Saran Das further expanded his business and commercial enterprises. Undertaking large contracts for the construction of a Division of the Nagda—Mathura Railway, he employed 12,000 men to complete the work. Perhaps due to the association of his father and later his own with the railways, Ram Saran Das developed a fetish for noting down the engine number of every train he travelled on.

Magnificent buildings, bridges and railway lines were also constructed by his firm, Messrs. R. B. Mela Ram & Sons, Lahore—named in the memory of his father.

Being a man of vision he also took an avid interest in public life. By the age of 22, he was nominated a member of the District Board Lahore, an office he held for 20 years.

He received great recognition at the hands of the government too. After inheriting a seat in Durbars, he attended Lord Elgin's Durbar held in Lahore and was a government guest at the Delhi Coronation Durbar and at the Durbar held by the Prince of Wales at Lahore in 1905. When the government appointed him as Joint-Secretary of the Kangra Valley Earthquake Relief Work in 1905, it is known that he rendered much valuable help in this crisis at his own cost. Years later in 1960, when the 14th Dalai Lama sought refuge in Dharamsala, he stayed initially in the hunting lodge that had belonged to R.B. Ram Saran Das, a property inherited by his third son, Ravi Shanker.

In 1906 he was exempted from the operations of the Indian Arms Act. The same year he was nominated a member of the Committee of Management, Government School of Engineering and of the Victoria Jubilee Institute in 1907.

He was a Municipal Commissioner for almost 18 years and in 1909, the title of 'Rai Sahib' was conferred on him.

The following year, in 1910 at the age of 34, he was elevated to the status of Rai Bahadur'. In 1913 he was elected to the Punjab Legislative Council where he was an active member. In 1914, he was awarded the Kaiser-i-Hind Gold Medal. In 1916 he was honoured with the 'C.I.E' (Commander of the Indan Empire). In 1920 R.B. Ram Saran Das came prominently into the limelight due to his election to the Council of State. With seven Hindu candidates of the province in the running for this coveted post and only one seat allotted to them, competition was stiff. To his credit his votes far surpassed those collectively of his rivals, resulting in his becoming a member of this prestigious body. He was elected to the Council of State under the Montford Reforms in 1920 at the age of 44.

CHAPTER IV

MANIFOLD ACTIVITIES OF R. B. RAM SARAN DAS AND REMINCESES

A man of exceptional energy, he was simultaneously involved in different fields. In 1933 he was the Northern India Chamber of Commerce delegate to the London Session of the Federated Chambers of the British Empire. He was also a government delegate to the Reserve Bank Committee which met in London and in 1937 was a delegate to the Empire Parliamentary Conference held in London.

At the All India Hindu Mahasabha session that opened in Lahore on 21st October 1936, Rai Bahadur Ram Saran Das, Chairman of the Reception Committee, in his welcome address said that the Hindu Mahasabha stood for the protection of the political rights of the Hindus and stressed upon the Hindus to remain united and self reliant.

He was the guest of the British Government in 1937, at the Coronation in London of King George VI and Elizabeth Bowes Lyon as King and Queen of the Dominion of the British Commonwealth and as Emperor and Empress of India at Westminister Abbey.

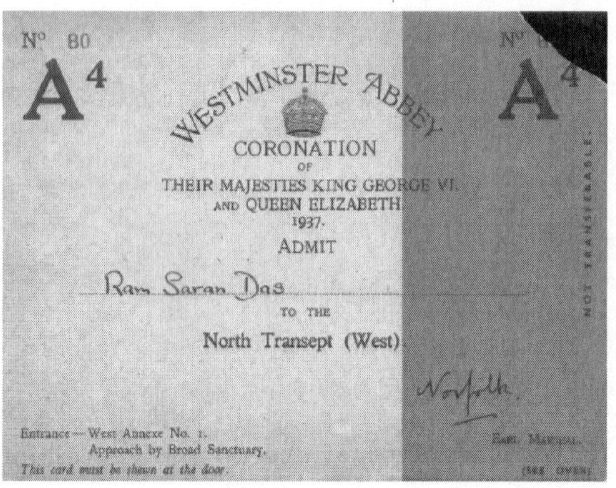

Nº 80

A 4

WESTMINSTER ABBEY

CORONATION

OF

THEIR MAJESTIES KING GEORGE VI.

AND QUEEN ELIZABETH.

1937.

ADMIT

Ram Saran Das

TO THE

North Transept (West).

Norfolk.

Earl Marshal.

Entrance—West Annexe No. 1.
Approach by Broad Sanctuary.

This card must be shewn at the door.

(SEE OVER)

NOT TRANSFERABLE.

Many societies and organisations honoured him with offices. He was President Punjab Sanatan Dharma Pratnidhi Sabha; All India Khatri Sabha; and being a landlord himself, a prominent member of All-India Land Holders Association.

Held in high esteem by the Commercial world, he was involved in diverse projects. Director Imperial Bank of India; Chairman, Advisory Committee of the Central Bank of India Ltd. (Punjab branches); Chairman Indian Institute of Bankers (Pb Branch); Vice Chairman, British India Corporation Limited, Cawnpore; Director, Trans-Continental Airways Ltd., Ex-Chairman Northern India Chamber of Commerce; Vice-Chairman, Gawaliar State Economic Board of Development; Member, Punjab Government Development Board; Director, Sutlej Cotton Mills Co. Ltd. And Chairman of the Sunlight of India Insurance Co. Ltd. Lahore.

Even when he visited cities in other states he was warmly received by local authorities, some of whom also honoured him with a civic reception. He was a member of various Standing and Select Committees for 30 years in the Provincial as well as in the Central Legislatures.

He held substantial shares in the Indian National Airways that plied on the Delhi-Lahore-Karachi sector of which Biju Patnaik, who later became Chief Minister in Orissa, was one of the pilots. He travelled within the country in his own plane to fulfil his many commitments. For their private use his two eldest sons Gopal Das and Rup Chand also had their own aircrafts, a French De Souter and a Leopard Moth. His second son, Rup Chand, set up the Lahore Flying Club.

Interested in the field of education, he donated the famous 'Peeli Kothi' which stood in front of Punjab University sports field for a college building. Initially it offered only graduate courses, but with changing times a post graduate curriculum was added.

When the Doon School in Dehra Dun celebrated its Golden Jubilee, the 50th anniversary of the school, the only surviving son of R.B. Ram Saran Das, my father's younger brother, Rajeshwar Bali Ram Saran Das, was specially invited to the event. He was informed that this was on account of his father being a Founding Member of the school.

The 'Article of Memorandum' of the school states that at the time of the establishment of the Doon School, there were ninety-eight Foundation Members. These were primarily rulers of princely states and leading figures from Delhi, Madras, Bombay, Bengal, United Provinces, Punjab, Central Provinces, Bihar and Orissa, N.W.F. Provinces and Indian States. Amongst them mentioned was R.B. Lala Ram Saran Das CIE from the state of Punjab.

Since childhood Ram Saran Das was deeply religious. His day commenced with prayers followed thereafter by religious rituals and meditation.

Interested in religious studies, he read in great detail the sacred books of the Hindus, but his preoccupation was not limited to the Hindu religion alone. He studied and contemplated deeply on the sacred books of the Muslims, Sikhs, Christians and other religions. He respected all religions and perhaps that is the very reason his approach to life was exceedingly tolerant and open. His non-communal outlook endeared him to all and he was popular with all communities.

According to an account written by Pt. Ram Lal Tara in a book, 'Punjab's Eminent Hindus,' Swami Ram Tirath, was a spiritual leader, whose interest was limited to matters concerning God. At a given time when the Swami was constantly changing his residential quarters, Ram Saran Das sought him out and requested him to be his spiritual guide. After some initial reluctance the Swami eventually agreed and moved to the comfort of his residence, the 'Lal Kothi.'

That Ram Saran Das enjoyed travelling, was very evident. He toured the length and breadth of India. In the Far East he visited the Dutch East Indies, Java, Bali, Malaya, Siam, Indo-China, Burma, Ceylon and in the Middle East, Egypt. All countries in Europe, apart from Russia, Sweden, Denmark, and Spain, were part of his excursions. During his travels, he always wore his traditional Indian dress, which consisted of an achkan, churidar pyjama and pugree. He and my grandmother travelled by ship and stayed in leading hotels with their entourage, which always included their personal staff and cooks. Love of travel took him to diverse corners of the globe and the experiences, undoubtedly, had a significant impact on both his outlook and thought.

Despite being a member of the Council of State, his commitment to his business and large land holdings remained unaffected. He was active and alert in matters related to his business and is reputed to have been 'far sighted with a sharp mind that was accurate like a mathematician' (P.D. Saggi). Be it in relation to matters at home, office or factory the smallest detail did not escape his attention. A connoisseur of Indian music he enjoyed classical music, art and ancient architecture. Intellectually, he was extremely knowledgeable on a variety of subjects and took pleasure in discussions with learned men. People enjoyed his company as his conversations were stimulating, lively and witty.

Compassionate and sensitive, he was careful not to hurt the sentiments and feelings of others. Exceedingly helpful, he found time to assist those in need, even if it involved travelling vast distances to solve their problems and never expected anything in return. Generous, he had a heart of gold and those who turned to him for help were never disappointed. He treated everyone with respect, regardless of age, status and religion and was loved by his vast domestic staff and not feared by them. What endeared him most to people was his humane approach towards his fellow beings.

In 1901, districts beyond the Indus River were separated from the state of Punjab, thereby creating a new state, the North-West Frontier Province. Fearing that the proximity to the Afghan and Persian borders would fuel Punjabi nationalism, the British introduced Urdu as the official language. It was originally the language of the soldiers and contained several Persian words. As the army was made up of Arabs, Turks and locals, Urdu became an amalgamation of all these languages. Once established as the language of literary expression in Punjab, Lahore became the centre of Urdu printing and publishing. However, with passing years and new influences, interest in the Urdu language waned. Ram Saran Das made generous donations for the publication of Urdu books and literary journals owned by Muslims, which were facing an acute financial crunch.

A great philanthropist, his charities exceeded over one million rupees. Educational institutions, hospitals and other public bodies were the primary beneficiaries of his largesse.

Keeping abreast with the times, he imported the very first car in Lahore from England. The arrival of the car together with the date and time was publicly announced. People were warned that as this vehicle did not give prior indication of its approach, there being no concept of a horn at that time, people had to be cautious. Lahore was agog to hear that a car had arrived and people lined up on the streets and crowded on balconies to see this mobile wonder move through their city. The car subsequently became the major topic of conversation. People worried about the danger this could pose and debated at length on the possibility of the vehicle endangering their lives. A solution, however, was eventually found and omission rectified regarding this major impediment. A man was appointed to run ahead of the car ringing a bell, so that people were forewarned. (Pran Seth has covered this in his article on the Lahorias on the Google.)

Kiran Tellis (youngest daughter of Gen. Pran Nath and Bimla Thapar) recalls what her maternal Grandmother (daughter of Harkishan Das married to R.B. Bashi Ram Sahgal) had told her. "She remembered her father (Harkishan Das, younger brother of Ram Saran Das) in particular. Being a crack shot, he taught Gopal Das (eldest son of R.B. Ram Saran Das) to shoot and gave him his first gun. Along with his elder brother's car also arrived a car for him and one for his two daughters which had curtains on the windows so they couldn't be seen. He also seems to have had rather an inflated opinion of himself and the family. When he was dying at the young age of 29 he said, "God has been unkind to me".

At a young age, after becoming the head of a large joint

family, Ram Saran Das took his responsibilities seriously. Following the death of his brother Harkishen Das, he became the inheritor of the family property, and took the two young daughters of his brother, Roop Kaur and Mohan Kaur, under his wing and brought them up as his own children.

It was not long before Ram Saran Das, moved to the Civil Lines, to a large mansion opposite the Falettis Hotel on Egerton Road. Here the entire extended family lived together under one roof. Each member of the family had a bedroom with an attached private sitting room and two attendants to take care of their needs. There were three kitchens, each serving Indian, vegetarian and continental cuisine to suit the palates of the occupants. The kitchens also had to cater to the constant entertainment hosted by the family. On more formal occasions food was served in thals and katoris of gold.

He maintained a huge establishment and a vast number of servants together with their families stayed on the premises. All requirements of the domestic staff were taken care of, and when any got married the entire expense was paid for.

The area of their residential premises covered 24 acres and being spacious, housed stables, cows, Victoria carriages and, later, cars.

Inderjit, his grandson, (son of R.B. Gopaldas) wrote about his grandfather in the following words, "Not only was he a nobleman, but also a big landlord, property owner and renowned foremost contractor. It was said he owned substantial property in Lahore as also numerous villages and 90 'murabbas' of land in Multan in the Montgomery district. His greatness was his humility and his philanthropy".

He also shared another anecdote, which he said was told to him by his father, R.B. Gopal Das, eldest son of Ram Saran Das. An erstwhile Maharaja of Guler from the Kangra state had commissioned a railway track to be made by Ram Saran Das. The Maharaja handed over a blank cheque to be filled once the work was complete. Ram Saran Das, uncomfortable with the concept of receiving a blank cheque replied, "Your Highness since you left the amount blank, it will remain blank". He ultimately laid the railway line at his own cost, without charging the Maharaja a penny. Inderjit claims he saw that blank cheque on a visit to the hunting lodge of his grandfather in Kangra, which was subsequently inherited by his elder brother Ripu Daman.

According to him Ram Saran Das used to move around ceremonially in a four horse carriage while the ladies and his sons in a two horse carriage and his grandchildren in a one horse carriage. The grandchildren were always accompanied by a valet even when they went to school. With the advent of motor cars, a fleet of cars were purchased for the use of the family. According to him the first telephone, first gramophone and the first motor car came to their household.

He said his father, (R.B. Gopal Das) got his first personal aircraft- Mark Desoutier, a French made 4 seater in 1923, and later his father's younger brother, Wing. Cmdr Rup Chand got a Leopard Moth, a De-Havilland built British 4 seater. J.R.D.Tata got his De Havilland Puss Moth in 1932. This is an indication of how advanced Lahore was at that time.

He recalls the musical programmes held at Edgerton Road where he remembers 'Tamancha Jaan', as being one of the regular performers. The mansion, with 35 rooms had four wings. In the centre was a courtyard—called 'wherra' in Punjabi where Bhayaji (Ram Saran Das) held musical concerts till his death in November 1945 due to a severe case of diabetes. He remembers it being a huge mansion and on visiting it in the early 1960's, the officer who took him on a detailed tour of "your magnificent house" , praised the quality and design of the house, adding, "I have not seen many such buildings. If I have my will, I will never allow it to be demolished as it's a showcase for all our corrupt and useless contractors". According to him, six offices were located on the premises.

My youngest uncle Rajeshwar Bali, recalling his youth in Lahore, gave glimpses of the life they led pre-partition.

Money was never handled directly by any family member and as nothing was denied them, they simply signed for any purchase made. He recalls seeing sacks of money being carried to the house, which were the rentals from various properties owned by the family.

As the three younger sons and older grandchildren of Ram Saran Das were around the same age, there was always a lot of activity in the house. He recalls how their many friends would get together fly kites and enjoy the varied facilities available on the premises—a swimming pool, tennis courts, a riding track a furlong away and a private airfield nearby.

The ladies of the family rarely went out. Socializing was limited to family and close friends. Neither did they visit the shopping centres. Instead shopkeepers brought rolls of material and jewellery to the house for them to buy. Their purchases made it worth their while.

According to Shobha Maini, the daughter of R.B. Gopal Das, the eldest son of Ram Saran Das, on the birth of a grandson a large amount of money was given in charity. The servants also got bonuses and additional new uniforms—white pyjamas and twill achkans for summer and khaki coloured achkans for winter.

Despite his busy schedule Ram Saran Das always made time for his younger grandchildren. According to Shobha, daily on return from school he would send for them and ask how they had fared and also took interest in their extra-curricular activities. Hoping to inculcate an interest in railways in their minds, perhaps due to the close connection that he and his father had with them, he invariably enquired how many trains they had seen whilst on a stroll along the famous canal in Lahore. They were taken regularly to Moghulpouara, a station near the Shalimar Garden, in a beige convertible Chevrolet, where they would compete with each other in noting down the numbers of the locomotives, primarily to please grandfather. On their return home he would instruct his servant, Lallu Shah, to give them a bowl of Kelloggs cornflakes.

She remembers how as a routine they would meet grandfather every Sunday. He would give the older grand children four annas while the younger were given two annas. Once a month, to the delight of the children, they were permitted to enter a room stacked with toys. Each child was asked to select something. The boys normally chose Meccano sets, rail tracks and engines and the girls, dolls and creative handwork. As this room was adjoining the entrance of the house she clearly remembers 'Babu' who sat at the entrance gate and announced names of each visitor entering the house.

One of Ram Saran Das' grandsons, (daughter Lalita's son) Tilak Puri, recalls an incident when he was nine years old. Expressing a desire to have a bicycle to his grandfather, he was overjoyed to find he was indeed the proud owner of one that same day.

My grand-father, I was told, loved children. He was very affectionate towards all his grandchildren and they on seeing him would go running towards him to be enveloped in a big bear hug. He always said he was happiest in their midst and was like a child himself in their company as he said they caused him the least trouble.

Shobha recalls how at the time of marriages, mundan ceremonies, or the very first time a child attended school, singers were invited to entertain people to mark the event. Being fond of music he often had Rasoolan Bai, the thumri singer to sing. These sessions lasted till mid-night. Children, though not allowed to attend these functions, would peep from the balconies overhead.

Large hearted and exceedingly generous, he ensured food was regularly given to the poor who would queue up daily outside the house. Nobody left hungry. In summer he would have Chabeels set up on the roadsides in Lahore for people to quench their thirst with a cold drink of lassi made of raw milk, sugar and water.

According to Shobha, my grandfather encouraged my grandmother, Paboji (as we all called her), to learn to play musical instruments and Rup Chand's wife, Villas Chachi, to sing the Meera Bai bhajans.

On October 30, 2017, 'The Tribune" newspaper in Chandigarh published the following under their heading—ON THIS DAY ...-HUNDRED YEARS AGO.

THE TRIBUNE

Lahore, Tuesday, October 30. 1917.

HINDU-MOSLEM CONCORD in LAHORE.

The happy scenes of deep and cordial good will which the capital of the Punjab witnessed during the Dussehra and Mohurrum constitute as much a feather in the cap of the two great communities as they indicate unmistakably a growing consciousness of the fact that the two communities must realise in an ever increasing degree the identity of their interest. The ball was set rolling on the day of the barat or marriage procession of Sri Ram Chandraji, when to the deep gratification of the Hindu residents, Nawab Fateh Ali Khan

Kazilhash, Khan Bahadur Sardar Mohammad Ali Khan, the Hon'ble K.B. Mian Muhammad Shafi, Khan Sahib Mian Syed Mohammad Amin Indrabi Municipal Commissioners and many other leading Mohammadans joined hands with Raja Narendra Nath and Hon'ble Rai Bahadur Ram Saran Das in looking to the starting of the Ram Lila procession, and most of them accompanied the procession throughout the route, in which the Mohammadans had improvised over a dozen places of entertainment for the benefit of their Hindu Brethren.

I sent the above reproduction from The Tribune to Syed Babar Ali, a highly successful Pakistani industrialist who set up the company, Packages Limited, was Finance Minister during the caretaker government in Pakistan and is the founder of the famous University, 'Lums' in Lahore, Pakistan.

His spontaneous response -

Thank you for sharing the Tribune article.

'I can myself recall the Zulganah procession on 10th of Mohurum before 1947 when elders of your family installed a Sabeel and themselves served water and milk to the participants on the street next to your Lal Kothi near Data Gangbaksh.'

Babar Ali, at my request sent some reminiscences of his association with the family.

Babar Ali recalled 'a grand function which I witnessed under the patronage of your grandfather, Rai Bahadur Ram Saran Das. This was the occasion of Suraj Shamsher's 'mundan' ceremony. (eldest son of Wing Cmdr. Rup Chand, the second son of the Rai Bahadur). The festivities lasted three days and the most prominent Indian classical singer, Kesar Bai Kerkar, was specially invited to Lahore to perform for the elite of the city. The next day there was a 'mujra' where famous singer, Noor Jehan, made her debut as a dancer and was known at that time as Baby Noor Jehan. Hundreds of prominent people of Lahore were invited to participate and Rai Bahadur Ram Saran Das hosted these festivities to commemorate an important milestone in the life of his grandson.'

Again he wrote;

I was in and out of your family home which was called, 'Manorma' on Egerton Road and spent much time with Suraj and Shakti's family. I recall meeting Rai Bahadur Ram Saran Das on some of my visits. He used to wear a Kashmiri shawl and always greeted me with 'Salam-o-Alaikum.' He was a friend of my father and particularly of my maternal grandfather, Faqir Syed Iftikharuddin who passed away in 1914.

My mother narrated to me that when Lala Gopal Das's wedding was to take place, Lala Ram Saran Das sent a message to my nana, Faqir Iftikharuddin, who was ailing at that time, that the marriage would only take place when he got better and could participate. My grandfather responded that a happy occasion should never be postponed and he urged Lalaji not to delay the wedding of his son. The barat went through Bazar-e-Hakeeman in Bhati Gate; the groom was mounted on an elephant, and my nana gave him salami.

The closeness of Syed Babar Ali and the sons of Rup Chand is evident from the piece below which is taken from Babar Ali's autobiography.

'My friend Suraj Shamsher with whom I maintained a very close relationship from my first day at school and whose parents and grandparents were close family friends, left for studies in Ohio in the summer of 1946. I went to see him off at Ballard Pier in Bombay. My father observed to my mother, 'Now we are in trouble! His friend has gone and now he will not stay here.

He again mentions his re-association with the two sons

of Roop Chand while studying in America at the University of Michigan, Ann Arbor and recalls;

'I went on a trip across the USA with my friend Suraj and his younger brother Shakti from the Mela Ram family of Lahore....we started on our journey in a new Packard convertible that Suraj had bought... motored from Columbus to Indianapolis, through Kansas city to Denver, Colorado, then onto Salt Lake City in Utah, through the Yellow Stone National Park and Glacier National Park and then to Seattle in Washington State. From there, we motored south along the Pacific coast to San Francisco and further on to Los Angeles, then on to Reno, Nevada, and from there to the Boulder Dam, then to Flagstaff in New Mexico and back to Denver. We travelled north to the Black Hills and Montana and then east to Chicago and further southeast, back to Columbus, Ohio, where we ended our trip.

The five week journey of almost 8,000 miles was a very educational experience, which not only taught us the geography of the United States but also introduced us to so many different people. We stayed mostly in small towns, in private homes and had the opportunity of living with lower middle class American families, who were very easy to get on with. They were kind and sympathetic to foreign travellers, but were very businesslike. This was a time when not many people from our part of the world had been to America and certainly not to the remote areas where we went. The scale of the country over-awed me. The ease with which we could travel, the people we met, and the way we were welcomed everywhere was just amazing. We did not feel discriminated against and we saw orderliness and activity everywhere. California impressed us the most because there was such tremendous prosperity there, even compared to elsewhere in America. However there was discrimination against the blacks, who were not even allowed to come and sit at a soda fountain. At that time, we were, in a way, used to such discrimination because in India we had encountered constant belittling prejudice by the British, while on the railway stations you had Hindu water and Muslim water', so we had been brought up with these sorts of barriers.'

On my request to Syed Babar Ali on March 6th, 2019 to give his perception of the contribution of my grand father to Lahore his following prompt response was received on 7th March, 2019.

Dear Nina

Delighted to hear from you and to learn that your book is ready for print.

As you know I have from early life been a devoted friend and admirer , as my elders were ,of your illustrious family.

To start with I heard from my mother the close relationship which her father Faqir Iftikharuddin(one time India's Agent,Ambassador,to Afghanistan in 1906-8).

When your Uncle's barat on an elephant went past his home in Bazar Hakiman Bhatti Gate(Lala Mela Ram's Katri was in the same street) Iftikharuddin gave salami as he was too ill to attend the wedding.

The first electricity plant in Lahore was at the Mela Ram Mills next to the shrine of Data Ganj Bakhsh and free lighting was provided by your grand father to the shrine.

He and later his sons set up a Sabile,offering refreshments, to the participants of 10th Mohurrum procession a prominent annual event in Lahore.He and his sons stood bareheaded to honour the Zulganah.

Lala Mela Ram donated over 30 Acres to the city of Lahore for the construction of the zoo.

These are some of the few legacies I learnt,

My wife and I are on a pilgrimage in Karbala Iraq and plan to return home on March 10.

I pray better sanity will prevail among our countries .

Lots of love to you and the family.
Babar

In December 2008 I had written a book 'A Life Across Three Continents' sub titled 'Recollections of a diplomats wife'. On reading the book, Gurbachan Singh, a former Indian Ambassador sent me a letter dated Sept. 24, 2010. The family house of Gurbachan Singh had been the residence of Pakistan's Head of Government in Rawalpindi for many years till the shift to the new capital, Islamabad. In the letter he wrote, "apart from other affinities, your father's family and ours were the two largest non-Muslim landowners in the Punjab." The largest of course were the Tiwanis; Gen Umar Hayat. His son Khizur was the last Prime Minister of undivided Punjab. Because he had stood steadfastly against partition and Jinnah, the new regime in Pakistan managed to completely destroy his family and dispossess them. His son, Nazar, ended up as a librarian in Chicago!

Relations between your parent's family and mine were close. Your grandfather treated my father more or less as a son. Your uncles, R.B. Gopaldas and Flt. Lt. Rup Chand were respectively, Tayaji and Chachaji to me unlike today's uncle. Worse, 'uncleji'!

Ram Saran Das was exceedingly hospitable and both

Congress leaders and members of the Royal families of India were frequently his house-guests. He followed the tradition of his father and had musical soirees at the Lal Kothi every Sunday. The illustrious list of invitees included Allama Iqbal, Sir Abdul Qadir, Raja Narindranath, Sir Umar Hayat Tiwana, Faqir Syed Iftikharuddin, Sir Sikander Hayat Khan, Sardar Joginder Singh, Raja Sir Daya Krishan Kaul, Nawab Liaquat Hayat Khan, Nawab Ahmed Yar Khan Daultana, Mir Mohammad Naziruddin Khan, Sardar Surjit Majithia, Syed Maratab Ali and Sir Shahabu Din amongst others. All were one happy group at that time and he was a generous and helpful friend.

> In the Council of State, Ram Saran Das expressed sorrow on the death of his close friend Malik Sir Umar Hyat Khan Tiwana, with the words,' I had the pleasure and privilege of knowing the late Major General Sahib for a long time. We were class fellows and came into contact with each other often. He was a great personality and a gallant soldier. We all mourn his loss and we wish that our condolences should be conveyed to his worthy son Colonel Malik Khizar Hayat Khan Tiwana and the family'.

Though he loved comfort and enjoyed life, in many ways he always remained at heart a simple man. His two elder sons, R. B. Gopal Das and Wing Cmdr. Rup Chand, were also known for their hospitality and generosity, thus following in their father's footsteps.

Hakim Ahmed Shuja, Secretary General of the United Punjab Legislature Assembly for over twenty years, giving a brief history of the prominent people of pre-partition Lahore wrote," Rai Bahadur Mela Ram and his son Ram Saran Das were great patrons of art and literature. Their social circle was vast and the whole nobility of that period was included in their functions that the family usually arranged in their Lal

Kothi. The building of Lahore railway station was constructed by Mela Ram and Mian Sultan. The account is before the family shifted to their new residence opposite Falettis hotel, Lahore. From the WAPDA building to Kashmir road (between Edgerton Road and the Mall the entire triangle belonged to the family. There were two hotels Metropole and Nedous (at the site of the present Hilton.)

Everyone loved and respected Ram Saran Das. His compassionate and humane qualities endeared him to both the rich and poor, and people of all communities as he never differentiated between them. As such he was looked up to by that generation of people. This trait appears evident in the following lines I found while surfing the net at random.

'Before the partition there used to live a very wealthy man near the shrine of Hazrat Dutta Gunj Baksh, Rai Bahadur Ram Saran Das. He was one of the richest men, among the wealthiest people of the United Punjab, and his generosity was incomparable. His philanthropist activities had treated the Hindus, Muslims, Sikhs and Christians equally '(From Face Book, sent by Usman Qazi to Mohammad Shahzed.)

The Dawn of 29, March,2004 in the Lahore number of the magazine 'Naqoosh' brought out an article by Shaikh Abdul Shakoor,'Kuch Ravadari Ki Baten" in which the author speaks of communal harmony of the years gone by and mentions specifically how R.B. Ram Saran Das had the Mazar of Data Sahib electrified.

During my husband and my second tenure in Pakistan, commencing in early 1992, I was presented a book 'From Memory' written by Sir Firoz Khan Noon, prime minister of Pakistan, by his Austrian wife, Lady Viqar un Nisa Noon. Here I found a reference to my grandfather. It is as follows--.

'Once I was told that a member (of the Council) at

Lahore who had forgotten to bring his own speech with him, just picked up his neighbour's and read it out quickly. The neighbour felt very embarrassed but held his peace, and when he, in his turn, was asked by Sir Michael O'Dwyer, the lieutenant governor, to express his views, he remarked, "I agree with my friend who has just spoken"'

The footnote said, 'The neighbour was Rai Bahadur Ram Saran Das. The other gentleman was a relation of mine, Sir Umar Hayat Tiwana'

Ram Saran Das had five sons and three daughters. His sons were Gopal Das, Rup Chand, Ravi Shanker, Jagdish Chander and Rajeshwar Bali. His daughters were Gopal Dei, Lalita Devi and Kans. The elder two sons and three daughters were from his first wife, Suraj Kanta. The latter three sons, Ravi Shanker, Jagdish Chander and Rajeshwar Bali were from his second wife, Amrit Kaur whom he married at a later age after the death of his first wife. The age difference between the elder five off-spring and the three youngest was considerable. In fact his younger sons were virtually the same age as his older grandchildren—the children of his elder two sons.

All the five sons and older grandsons of Ram Saran Das studied in Aitchison School and all wore the traditional Indian costume—achkan, churidar pyjama and pugree, to school. Initially they went to school in a buggy drawn by horses, but once motor cars made an entry into Lahore, my uncle Rajeshwar recalls, they were driven in a seven seater Fiat wagon. However, during the war years, owing to rationing of petrol, they reverted to travelling by one-horse drawn Victoria carriages. There were governesses to look after the granddaughters and all were educated in English medium schools and colleges.

The Scottish born Lieutenant Governor of Punjab, Sir

Charles Umpherston Aitchison, founded Aitchison School for boys in 1886. Later it came to be referred popularly as Chiefs College as it was established to educate the sons of Punjab's Chiefs and Landlords. Initially admission was very restricted, being confined only to those families mentioned in the Punjab Chiefs Book. But with only forty students and sixty teachers they realised some rectification had to be made to make the education system of the school more meaningful. At a given point, the Maharaja of Patiala took over the responsibility of getting students from influential families of the Punjab. Due to the practice of early marriages, a few students were already married when they joined.

Set up on 150 acres of land, the school had three boarding houses, a mosque, a temple, a gurdwara, a playing field, parade ground, riding school, gymnasium, dairy farm and a hospital. The Principal, always an Englishman, resided behind the main building. There were a large number of British teachers. Emphasis was on discipline, acquiring knowledge, being groomed for good behaviour, to be truthful, humble and modest. A typical day started with physical training in the morning, followed by studies and compulsory games in the afternoon. Evenings were for prayers. Sundays were not free.

There were not many students and as each class had no more than ten to twelve students, close bonds of friendships were formed. Primarily a boarding school, residents of Lahore were not permitted to be day scholars. The only exceptions were the sons of Sardar Baldev Singh, the then Indian Defence Minister and Sir Khizar Hayat Khan, then Chief Minister of Punjab. In the case of Ram Saran Das it pertained to his sons and grandsons.

As students from Punjab increased, there were many more boarders. Facilities provided for the boarders were excellent. Initially each student had a separate bedroom, a bath and a dressing room with a personal attendant provided by the school. Meals were also of a high quality. Thus, living conditions for boarders were considered to be luxurious. But towards the late 30's, the British principal, Berry, opened the doors to all for admission, thereby enrolling many more students. With this influx, two or three boarders now had to share a bedroom and one attendant was considered sufficient for all three. Earlier, a Chiefs College Diploma was presented to each student on graduating, but later a Senior Cambridge certificate was given. The fees were ₹105 per month.

In his autobiography, 'Learning from Others,' Babar Ali recounts, "We were a hundred odd students at Aitchison and everybody knew everybody. Among my first friends at Aitchison were Suraj Shamsher, son of Lala Rup Chand of the distinguished Mela Ram family of Lahore, and his younger brother Ranbir Shamsher. Ranbir died while at school after an appendix operation. This was the first death of a student at Aitchison while I was there and it was a traumatic experience because the entire school followed the funeral procession from the family house on Edgerton Road on foot to the cremation ground outside Taxali Gate, a distance of over three miles. It was very sad to see a dear friend's body engulfed in flames; the pyre was lit by his unfortunate father.

Recalling incidents of the past, he wrote to me, "I particularly remember a Russian circus that came to Lahore and occupied a property belonging to your family off Abbot Road. While the circus was still in Lahore, it went bankrupt and was unable to pay the rent. As compensation, your family received a horse from the circus and I remember your father and uncle bringing that grey horse for riding at Aitchison College. The horse was so well trained that as soon as the bell went, it started to dance. This is something I can still remember very vividly."

All five sons and grandsons later studied in Government College, Lahore. The fee for Government College was ₹28 per month. This was a prestigious intellectual centre where students were considered to be the best representatives of modern education. The standard of education was high. Priority for admission was given to agricultural families of Punjab. Babar Ali, however, in his book describes the transition from Aitchison to Government College as 'going from a 5-star to a 2-star hotel.' He adds, "the most important differentiating feature between the two institutions was the varied background of the students. At Government College students came from different schools, varied walks of life and spoke different languages. The boys from Aitchison and the Doon School had a different standard of conduct and treated the staff with more respect. The students from these two schools hung together rather than socialize with the rest".

The Government College, founded in 1864, was one of the oldest universities and its emblem represented the Light of Knowledge. Its motto was, 'Courage to Know.' A picturesque building with a large central clock tower, it was built in a soaring Gothic style and had large verandahs and high ceilings. Architecturally, the college was striking and a landmark in the city—a red building with Lahori bricks, black Chiniot stone for the first floor columns and slate for the roof from the mountains of Dalhousie.

In the 1940's G.D. Sondhi was the principal of the college. The professors were of a high calibre with Oxford and Cambridge backgrounds. Dressed in black gowns, they delivered lectures and some encouraged open discussions, making the studies more gripping and interesting. Besides studies, it had extra curricular activities such as sports, debates, drama, music and the game of bridge. There was, significantly, no communal divide, and the atmosphere was cosmopolitan. Jinnah and the Muslim League had not made any breakthrough in Punjab, yet. All students lived together in the college hostel. despite there being separate kitchens for the Muslim and Hindu boarders. Inspite of all these restrictions, the students freely exchanged dishes with each other.

Accused of producing idle and extravagant students, a columnist likened Government College pupils to coloured butterflies, "squandering the hard-earned money of their parents on frivolous pursuits, setting a bad example for the student community of Lahore and making a nuisance of themselves by a vulgar display of snobbery". Contrary to this criticism, however, Government College produced some of the most outstanding ICS and IFS officers and journalists.

On my first visit to Lahore in 1978 I was taken to see the mansion opposite the Falettis Hotel where the family had resided on Edgerton Road. It was by then a government office for the Rehabilitation of Enemy Property. Some wings of the house, I was told, had been demolished to make way for new roads. There was no sign of the four wings Inderjit (son of R.B. Gopal Das) had mentioned. At that point of time the existing rooms had been subdivided into cubicles for office use and visualising it as a home was difficult. The marble staircase was the only visible evidence of a glorious era gone by. The building itself was dirty and poorly maintained, but traces of its once being a beautiful mansion remained. Much later on a brief visit in 2015, I found a totally new building constructed on the same premises of the old house. Nearby was the WAPDA building, which I was told, had been built on the premises of the demolished Mela Ram Building.

CHAPTER V

LAHORE AND POLITICS DURING THE TIME OF R.B. RAM SARAN DAS

Till the advent of the 20th century the people of Lahore showed little interest in national politics. Yet with the sequence of unfolding events, Lahore came to hold a special position in both the history of the Pakistan Movement and the Indian Independence Movement. The economic, religious, social and cultural metamorphosis over the past decades had a direct impact, creating a new awareness. Atrocities on the locals by the British were followed by agitations in different parts of the country. With its immediate neighbouring city Amritsar, being a target of brutality at Jallianwala Bagh, it was impossible for Lahore to remain unaffected and it was soon sucked into the whirlpool of politics.

The milestone meeting of the Indian National Congress in 1885 was the first concrete step taken to voice dissent against the British. It was founded primarily by the western educated elite to enable them to achieve the following aspirations—to compete in the Indian Civil Service which till now had only been a white man's domain; tariff protection for their fledgling industries and relief for the peasantry who were oppressed by high revenue demands.

In 1905, as emotions peaked, Lord Curzon, the Viceroy

and Governor General, ordered the partition of Bengal, with the Eastern Areas being Muslim and the western areas, Hindu. He justified this unprecedented decision on the grounds that it would lead to improvement in the administrative efficiency of the state. In reality this was in keeping with their policy of divide and rule. The British feared the two communities would join hands to oust them and this was a decisive move to divide the Hindus and Muslims. This outraged the Bengalis and was met by stiff opposition from the Indian National Congress. The partition was finally annulled and Bengal was again unified half a decade later in 1911. However, with this act the first seeds of Hindu-Muslim disharmony were sown by consciously dividing them into two distinct communities.

In 1906 the Muslim League was formed primarily to protect the interests of the Muslims and act as an opposition to the National Congress. Despite their differences, the Muslim League, more than often, agreed with the Congress in matters of mutual interest, as their common agenda was to expel the British from India. The Muslims being a minority were apprehensive, believing they would have no say in a Hindu dominated India. Insecurity, articulated by Muslim intellectuals, led to the birth of the concept of the two nation theory. The British encouraged this thinking and worked surreptitiously to pit one community against the other, thereby following a policy to suit their own interest—one that eventually succeeded.

At the end of World War I, the process of urbanisation sped up. A large number of soldiers migrated to Lahore to take advantage of the educational and health facilities and other modern amenities. Post World War I, the Indians had hoped that after their supportive participation in the war on the side of Britain, where thousands of Indian soldiers had sacrificed their lives, the British attitude towards them would change. But this did not happen. The situation remained the same as the British continued to exploit the ground situation to their advantage.

The lavish lifestyle the British enjoyed at the cost of exploiting the country and their open disdain towards the Indians was taking its toll. Education had produced thinking students who had access to a wider spectrum of perceptions. Having reached a saturation point with the policies of the British, the Indians retaliated. 1900-1929 proved to be turbulent years. The India National Congress in Punjab, the Non Cooperation Movement and the Martial Law agitation attracted a large number of students. Various agrarian protests followed, including opposition to the Punjab Land Alienation Bill in 1900 and Punjab disturbances in 1907. The Rowlatt Act, which subsequently gave the government power to indefinitely extend emergency measures of preventing indefinite detention without trial, further incensed the people. This led to the Jallianwala Bagh incident in Amritsar in 1919 when the British army, under the orders of Brigadier Reginald Dyer, opened fire without any provocation, against the gathering celebrating Baisakhi and simultaneously protesting against the policies imposed. This resulted in the massacre of a thousand unarmed men, women and children.

Meanwhile separate electorates were created for Hindus, Muslims and other communities, encouraging Muslims to develop as a socio-cultural group. The Indian Council Act of 1919 reserved 30% of the seats for Muslims. Gandhi's Satyagraha and the freedom struggle had an impact which had its own reverberations. In 1928 no Indian was included in the Simon Commission set up to examine potential constitutional arrangements. With the turmoil encircling it, Lahore could not remain unaffected and soon found itself embroiled in national politics.

In 1929, the historic Indian National Congress session declared full independence as its goal. A resolution was passed unanimously on the midnight of 31st December 1929, when Jawahar Lal Nehru, as the young President, proclaimed 26 January as the Republic Day. On this important occasion, the contemporary tricolour was hoisted as a national flag and thousands saluted it proudly. This was followed by the 240 miles Dandi March led by Gandhiji, to protest against the tax on salt. Simultaneously a Swadeshi exhibition whose purpose was to promote national industries and give a call to boycott foreign goods took place. The British realising that this would hurt their authority and economic interests dealt with the protests with a heavy hand. Fuelling the already simmering anger, this period also marked the beginning of critical journalism. The venue of all political meetings was the Mochi Gate while political debates were held at Bradlaugh Hall.

When the 1935 Act was formulated, the provincial government was established and the premier of Punjab was Sikander Hyat Khan. The revenue minister was Chota Ram who was also responsible for all the agricultural reforms in Punjab.

In September 1939, Viceroy Linlithgow, without consulting the Provincial governments, declared India's entry into the war against Nazi Germany.

The outbreak of World War II changed the fortunes of many. It was believed that the greatest industrial development occurred during this time as a considerable number of new industries came into being on account of war demand. The economic depression of the 1930s gave way to abundant job opportunities. Railway engineering activities expanded rapidly to meet the need of the hour. Goods constantly required for the war effort were supplied to the military, resulting in a phenomenal increase in business and production. The status of Lahore was enhanced as it became recognized as the new commercial and manufacturing centre of Punjab.

With an increased demand for recruitment to the army, people of all classes and religions joined the forces making it the most sought after profession. Two and a half million soldiers from India were sent to fight the war. In Europe they fought against Germany and Italy and in South Asia against Japan, eventually liberating Singapore and Hongkong, following the Japanese surrender in 1945. Over 87,000 Indian soldiers died during the war. Field Marshal Auchinlock, Commander in Chief of the Indian Army in 1942, acknowledged that Britain " couldn't have come through both wars (World War I and II) if they hadn't had the Indian army"

The Muslim League supported the war efforts, but the Indian National Congress demanded independence as a pre-condition. Moreover the educated Hindus began raising questions on constitutional matters. This led to distrust and hostility towards the Congress, while the stance towards the Muslim League became more partial.

The years 1938 -45 witnessed an increase in the demand for an independent India by the Indian National Congress with a simultaneous demand for a separate Muslim state. The Quit India movement in 1942 led by Gandhiji, resulted in thousands being imprisoned. The Congress Working Committee members were taken to Ahmednagar Fort.

The imprisonment of Gandhiji and Congress leaders en masse created a political vacuum, of which Jinnah and the Muslim League took political mileage. The most important resolution passed by the premier party, All India Muslim League, later known as the Pakistan Muslim League, was for the creation of a separate state for Muslims of India to be called Pakistan. This resolution was adopted in its session held in March, 1940 under the leadership of Muhammad Ali Jinnah who publicly proposed the two-nation theory for the first time. Economic disparity between the three communities, Hindus, Sikhs and Muslims, created a political program for the Muslim League to raise issues like repression of Muslim masses and the need for the creation of Pakistan for the benefit of the Muslim community.

The Quaid-e-Azam's demand for a separate homeland did not come as a surprise. It succeeded overnight in dividing people of Punjab, who had lived, played, studied and worked together for centuries. The tranquil life of the city was shattered with the communal divide and the rumblings of the partition.

Lahore has many associations with the Freedom Struggle. Both the call for Purna Swaraj (complete independence), made at the Congress session in December 1929, and The Resolution, demanding the creation of Pakistan, passed in 1940 were made at Lahore. The city is also closely associated with the legendary freedom fighter Bhagat Singh.

THE AFTERMATH OF WORLD WAR 2

The British came initially as traders to India in 1600. Of the 336 years of British presence, authority was exerted for 190 years. Following the 1757 Battle of Plassey, Warren Hastings, on becoming Governor, expanded their trade empire, leading to the formation of the East India Company, which remained in control till 1858, a period of 101 years. From 1858-1947 the British Crown ruled for the next 89 years. Over three centuries of economic exploitation, together with the discriminating and suppressive stance of the British towards the Indians, gradually took its toll, leaving them no choice but to grant independence to their prized colony.

The lifestyle of the British in India is apparent from the observation made by Edward VIII, during his stay with Lord Lloyd, the Governor of Bombay. He said he had never known what authentic regal pomp really meant until now. Yet the standard the Governor maintained was nothing compared to the opulent lifestyle of the Viceroy in Delhi. Sir Edwin Landseer Lutyens lived up to his promise to create an edifice that would evoke both awe and majesty. The compound was huge, 330 acres of land and housed 6,000 servants and their families. Cars, horses, two special trains and aeroplanes were at the disposal of the Viceroy. British extravaganza was matched by that of the Indian princes, who spent lavishly on palaces, hospitals and universities. As such, they were wooed by the British as natural rulers of Indian society.

Relations between the British and Indian princes were determined through treaties, keeping British interests paramount with restrictions imposed on the princes. For the six hundred odd princes a hierarchy was established through a gun salute which was tabled from 9 to 21. Banners and a Coat of Arms too were created to give each a distinct identity. Princes with gun salutes higher than 13, had the privilege of being addressed as 'His Highness.'

While the British kept control of foreign relations and defence, the princes were permitted to collect revenue and administer justice within their state. The British retained overall authority through the right to advise the ruler, to decide on a successor to the throne and to intervene in conflicts between rulers. Princes were obliged to keep Imperial Service

Troops and pay for their maintenance, the cost of which was quite staggering. By 1931 the British troops numbered 60,000.

In acknowledgement of the support by the princes in World War 1, Lord Chelmsford convened the first Princes Conference in 1916. This took a constitutional form through the establishment of the Chamber of Princes inaugurated in 1921. The rapid infrastructural developments together with social and economic changes taking place, led to a political awakening and a greater demand for a share in power and economic resources.

In the aftermath of war, the British, due perhaps to proximity to the oil fields in the Middle East, played a communal card in order to have a continued presence in the area. A rift was created by patronising a part of the population, granting land to those who supported them and exploiting political ambitions of aspiring individuals. Their policy to encourage a Hindu-Muslim divide is best described in the words of Winston Churchill that 'the united communities joining' could show them the door. He announced that he had not become the King's first minister to preside over the liquidation of the British Empire. A well thought over decision regarding the partition of Bengal, encouraging the setting up of the Muslim League and having separate electorates, resulted ultimately in the partition of the country, showcasing the success of their divide and rule policy.

Simultaneously, changes took place in Britain too. Prime-minister Winston Churchill suffered a crushing defeat and the Labour Party, under the leadership of Prime-minister Atlee, came to power. The new government on viewing the gravity of the situation granted India its freedom in 1947. This resulted in the partition of India into two sovereign countries, India and Pakistan. Lahore became a part of Pakistan in 1947, after having been the capital of undivided Punjab for centuries.

Though colonial rule made strides in material progress, it simultaneously enhanced awareness of communal identities causing a divide. Nonetheless, the British left a legacy in the Indian subcontinent, in the form of the English language, the Parliamentary system of government, the legal structure, the bureaucracy and the civil services.

CHAPTER VI

The Punjab Legislative Council.

R.B. Ram Saran Das was active in political life at a young age. He had been a Municipal Commissioner before he became a member of the Punjab Legislative Council.

Having the authority to make laws, the Punjab Legislative Council consisted of both official and non-official members with a term of three years. R.B. Ram Saran Das, as an active member of the Punjab Council, took his role seriously and the questions he put forth were an indication of his concerns.

His queries related to various subjects—expenditures incurred of various Public Work; schemes and amounts spent on metalled roads by Public Works Department and district boards; application of Civil Service Regulations retirement rules to Sub Registrars aged 55 or over 60 years; appointments of district board Engineers and the assignment of Imperial recurring grant to Primary education.

Balance of wheat for consumption in the Province after deducting exports; expenditure of wheat profits; total production of wheat from Punjab during 1917 and the supply falling short of demand.

He recommended conferences for 1) distribution of educational grants to local bodies and 2) to advise the Government of India on recommendations of Public Service Commissions. His queries pertained to consolidated grants to district boards and their effect; development grants;

withdrawal of existing grants from district boards; reduction of maintenance charges of district boards; the new maintenance charges imposed on them and objections by district boards regarding new schemes of consolidated grants.

It also included the distribution of land for grazing cattle in new colonies and questioned the killing of agricultural cattle because of their hides; effect of fixed grants on opening of new Primary schools; fees in district board primary schools; grants to local boards for schools; new primary schools; imperial grant for improving pay of teachers and provincial grants for the improvement of Primary education.

He enquired about the election in trans-Indus Municipalities and the increase of non-official members in certain municipalities. He was involved in the encouragement of Co-operative Societies among the industrial classes.

He desired an expenditure of imperial grant of 19 lakhs for education and sanitation; expenditure of non-recurring grants for sanitation; increase in grants for sanitation. He questioned Non-recurring imperial grant on education; Provincial grants for educational institutions; Provincial grants for local bodies for vernacular education; raising the Rasul Engineering School to the status of a College and the opening of separate institutions for teaching Unani and Ayurvedic systems of medicine.

Questions were raised regarding land revenue income and expenditure; local opinion in regard to liquor shops; notified areas and municipalities; overseers from Roorki and Rasul. Provincial Service-Officers as Under-Secretaries; rights in trees in Kangra; stoppage of grain compensation allowances; supply of detailed Civil Estimates; temporary overseers and permanent appointments; war allowance to low paid clerks of Government; water logging in Lahore; grain compensation allowance and a fuller explanation of the Revised Financial Statement.

His multiple interests concentrated primarily on issues such as local self government, rural education and sanitation. His views regarding public health were expressed in the following words-

"Your Honour, in all civilised countries Public Health is a great national asset. In modern days of stress and strife every unit of the commonwealth must conserve its manpower, not only to serve the British Empire in time of War, but also to improve and strengthen its economic and material output in times of peace....It is therefore, not only the interest of the people, but also of the Government to adopt every possible measure for the protection, conservation and development of manpower......our sanitary and medical establishments should leave no stone unturned to improve Public Health for it is only healthy members of a nation who can do anything..."

Surfing through Google I found the following extracts pertaining to R.B. Ram Saran Das from 'The Tribune" under the heading -100 years ago, referring to his years in the Legislative Council. These are re-produced below-

In their 1oo years ago

The Tribune Chandigarh India

April 16, 2014

Although the British Government does not openly acknowledge the fact, yet the Native States of India exert a powerful influence on the policy of the Government. The Hon'ble R.B. Ram Saran Das will ask questions with regard to preparation of programmes of sanitary projects by district boards and minor.

The Tribune, Lahore, Friday May 15, 1914 reported the following.

"At the last meeting of the Punjab Legislative Council, the Hon'ble R.B. Ram Saran Das raised the question of 'the tension of feeling between the two great sister communities of the province—the Hindus and Mohommedans". The gulf between the two communities was, he said, 'widening everyday'. Under the circumstances while the people could make no united efforts in the paths of progress, the Government also found obstacles in their way. He quoted Sir John Hewatt who had declared that' the wider the gulf, the more difficult it became to bridge over. The more severe the wound, the deeper has the surgeon's knife to penetrate and longer does it heal'. He suggested that the local officers should foster feelings of brotherliness at such places by forming Conciliation Boards".

The Tribune Lahore, March 21, 1915 reported:

Jhang Hindu deputation

An important deputation of several leading Hindus waited on His Honour the Lieutenant Governor at Government House on Saturday forenoon to lay before His Honour the suffering of the distressed Hindus in parts of the Jhang district, who have badly suffered during the recent rebellion of lawlessness. The delegation consisted of the following gentlemen. The Honourable R. B. Ram Saran Das ...."

The Tribune Lahore, Saturday, September 1915 reported.

The Punjab Legislative Council

Rai Bahadur Ram Saran Das has tabled 26 questions several of which are of pressing importance. He asks for information on the supply to Bikaner of the waters of the Sutlej river for purposes of irrigation and calls attention to the practice of restricting admission to the first year class of the Lahore Government College to the First Division students and asks the government whether it proposes to strengthen the staff and increase the accommodation of that college. He asks the Government to inform the Council of the trend of its reply to the Supreme Government about the allotment of lands to Indian soldiers and the locality and extent of land reserved.

The Tribune Lahore, Saturday, August 5, 1916 mentions that the Lieutenant Governor gave a speech on Hon'ble Rai Bahadur Ram Saran Das's resolution.

The Tribune of Tuesday August 11, 1998 has in its 75 years ago reported----

HINDU-SIKH SHRINE CLAIMS

The Punjab Swarakshs Sabha in its meeting held last week resolved that the Hon'ble Rai Bahadur Ram Saran Das CIE and Professor Gulshan Rai be nominated on their behalf to cooperate with two nominees of the Shironami Gurdwara Parbandhak Committee.

CHAPTER VII

COUNCIL OF STATE

R.B. Ram Saran Das was the only individual to have been a member of the Council of State for a quarter of a century since its inception in 1921 till his death in 1945.

Created by the Government of India Act 1919, The Council of State, the Upper House of the Legislature, was the predecessor to the current Rajya Sabha. Initially, it was constituted of 60 members of which 26 were nominated and 34 elected for a term of five years.

The elected members were appointed from Madras, Bombay, Bengal, United Provinces, Punjab, Bihar and Orissa, Central Provinces, Burma and Assam with elections held every five years. Women were not permitted to be members. To qualify for elections, members had to fulfil any of the following conditions --1) Pay an annual income tax of ₹10.000 or annual revenue of ₹750. 2) Be a Member of the Senate or of a University. 3) Have experience in any Legislative Council or 4) be a Title holder.

Punjab had a representation of four seats in the Council of State. Two, reserved for Muslims from East and West Punjab, one for a Sikh candidate and the fourth a general seat. R.B. Ram Saran Das consistently won the election on the only general seat.

The first session was held on Thursday, 3rd February, 1921 when all members of the Council took oath. The Duke of Connaught presided over the inaugural ceremony, on February 9, 1921.

The first commencement of the Council of State was followed by the second in 1926, the third from 1930-36 and thereafter the fourth. Ram Saran Das had the unique distinction of being the only member who continuously remained a member through all successive Councils, until his death in November 1945. During his last seven years he was the Leader of the Opposition in the Council of State.

An active participant in the Council from the beginning, Ram Saran Das's initial intervention on the first day was in regard to the importance of the Upper House. He strongly believed that it should not be influenced by what was passed elsewhere and was in agreement with another member that repressive laws should not be imposed on the public.

His speeches depicting his views in every session, reinforced with substantive facts and figures, were received favourably by all.

Accessing the proceedings of the Council of State was not easy as these have not been digitised in the Rajya Sabha records. I was, however, able to access discussions from the inception of the Council of State in the early 1920's and the last seven years of his membership from 1938-1945. I was also fortunate to get the proceedings of the Council in the early 1930's from Google. Thus my coverage is for 15 out of the 25 years of his membership. He made long interventions on topical subjects of the day. His speeches are a reflection of him as a man of extraordinary vision, far sighted, public spirited, humane and concerned with the larger national good.

Over the years, due to their close interactions, strong bonds were formed amongst the members of the Council of State. In 1988, whilst on a visit to Budapest where my husband was then posted, M.A. Chidambaram recalled how his father, Annamalai Chettiar (also a member of the Council), had sent him to the Amritsar border with funds, for the immediate use of the Ram Saran Das family in the aftermath of partition in 1947. However, he was unable to locate any member amongst the surging crowd of refugees and returned to Madras with his mission unfulfilled. In view of the gravity of the situation his father had attempted to assist the family of his friend.

Extracts of some important statements made by Ram Saran Das on topical subjects in the Council of States between 1920 and 1945

His focus in the debates of the Council of State for an uninterrupted quarter century provided an insight of his priorities and interests as indicated below.

FISCAL ECONOMY

Making fiscal autonomy the centerpiece of his interventions on financial and economic policies Ram Saran Das said, "Fiscal autonomy is essential to India if she is to be called upon to take a worthy part in the Common Wealth of the British Empire."...adding "the Government of India should be free to arrange and re-arrange its tariffs in anyway best suited to the conditions of India. If we get freedom in building and pulling down our tariffs walls in a way we chose to do, we will be killing not two but many birds with one stone."

"By getting fiscal autonomy we can, by arranging tariffs... give protection to such struggling indigenous industries that cannot at present stand against free trade competition of the West. We can at the same time set up and build up new industries under the protection of tariff walls of desirable heights"..."Fiscal autonomy would make us stand upon our own legs, would cause us to stand with our heads erect among the self-respecting nations of the world, and would make us feel that we are a free and equal partner in the commonwealth of British nations...I earnestly hope that England will not, at this critical juncture in the history of the world, be guided by the short-sighted policy and self-seeking interests of some of her industrial and commercial classes".

RAILWAYS

From the very onset, due to the close connection he and his father, R.B. Mela Ram, had over the years with the railways, he showed special interest in affairs pertaining to it. In the 1920's he raised questions regarding Railway Mail Service Offices and the problems faced by the postal strike in Punjab and concern whether "in the recent revision of salary, increase has been given to the clerical and menial postal staff in proportion to the rise in prices and cost of living?'

By compelling the government to disclose the number of Indians in the senior staff it was revealed that at the level of Inspectors, 27 posts were held by Europeans, 20 by Anglo-Indians and 7 by Indians. Similarly in respect of Station Masters, 115 posts were held by Europeans, 64 by Anglo-Indians and 39 by Indians (as on February 28, 1921).

In the 1930's, claiming that he travelled 3,000 miles per month by rail his information was 'that out of ₹31 crores income from passenger fares, ₹27 crores come out of the pockets of third class passengers' who deserved better. He bemoaned that 'unsanitary conditions of latrines for long distance journeys....inadequate waiting sheds and separate waiting halls for ladies and the extinguishing of lights to save oil created a security hazard'... 'conditions in rural areas, as far as safety is concerned, are going from bad to worse' and suggested that the Government should 'increase the second class accommodation' as 'they would get much more income without these new surcharges.'

Objecting to a single contractor getting the monopoly of food supply on trains, he mentioned the name when challenged. 'When Government accepts half a lakh or more from one contractor, that money has to come out of the pockets of the travelling public. With absence of competition the poor people suffer,' adding that though the conditions did not permit subletting, the contractor was doing so in violation of this rule. When members were articulating doubts on the pricing of the variety of food served, his one word intervention 'Pure,' revealed his emphasis was mainly on quality. He exhibited at times a sense of humour when he said that instead of using pure ghee, food was made of substances which created ' a suffocating sensation in your throat' leading to laughter in the House.

He objected to 'the reduction in the salaries and allowances of journey men. Hitherto their salary was ₹100 per month. Journeymen are those technical people who qualify themselves from the technical colleges and join the workshops. When the Railways realised that a number of men were coming forth...the scale of salaries and allowances were reduced to ₹75 a month. Now I think it is ₹60....That on the face of it is wrong in principle'

Speaking on the Railway Budget in 1930's, he was critical of the enhancement of the fare and freight and the reduction of staff and cut in salaries. Railways, he said, had created a rival for themselves through lorry traffic. In times of unemployment he was opposed to reduction of staff, stating, 'although in England we see riot after riot taking place in regard to this very question, the matter is not even being properly considered in India.' Describing reduction in salary as a 'vicious blunder', he said the 'railways are run on business lines and we should treat them in a business-like manner.'

In 1941, while congratulating the Railway Minister and the Chief Commissioner for Railways for 'getting such an unprecedented surplus in railway income (₹6 ¼ crores) he expressed disappointment that railways were given only ₹19,000 to improve amenities.

On the dismantling of railway lines he queried, '... the railway authorities say that some of these lines were superfluous and others were unremunerative and therefore they are being dismantled. I would like to know who was responsible for putting up these unremunerative and superfluous lines? Why was India's money so recklessly wasted?....If these lines remained here till the end of the war, they will not have inconvenienced the public, who have been accustomed to the convenience of railway travel. ...that Provincial Governments are consulted with all deference, is untrue. I find that the Bengal Minister for Communications strongly protested against the dismantling of the Kalukahali Bhatipara line. Two Ministers came to Delhi to put their grouse before the authorities, but they were told that Government had already arrived at a decision.'

Advisory Committees he lamented used to meet once a month, but now these meetings had been fixed quarterly. 'That means that...the utility of these Committees is being minimized.'

Concerned about the plight of the poor and low paid staff of the railways he said, 'We agitated for the revision and reduction of the pay and allowances of the superior services. But we never meant that the pay and allowances of the low paid staff should be revised and decreased.' That is why when applications are invited for train clerks, response is meagre and there are very few who apply.'

Due to the huge surplus, he requested that 'some relief be given to the tax-payer,....those who make contributions to your income must have some amenities and I find that the amenities so far given are practically nothing and I am rather distressed....' With increase of fares he asked if lighting the railway coaches was on the agenda

As regards measures taken against ticketless travellers and with increase in 'many penal laws, murders, theft, dacoities and other crimes,' he suggested introduction of 'corridor carriages and ...a ticket collector or checker on every train.' He advised during a period of an epidemic, ...a big placard should be placed at the railway station of the city affected, to warn people, adding there ought also to be separate compartments segregating those suffering from highly infectious diseases.

Regarding racial discrimination he said, ...' Queen Victoria gave a Magna Charta to India when she among other things proclaimed that in the services there will be no distinction of caste, colour or creed. I deplore that a communal policy was accepted by the Government of India. In commercial departments, efficiency must be the chief factor on which recruitment should be based,' adding 'Where is the justification of maintaining the percentage of Anglo-Indians at the expense of Indians' adding 'now Indian Christians and others are classified as Indians...'

In the 1940's, regarding manufacturing of railway locomotive engines, he regretted the decision of the Government...to not start the manufacture of locomotives in India on a reasonable scale. 'I find they have given a small order to the Ajmer workshops for a small number of locomotives. That is simply eyewash. When Government are spending huge sums of money in time of war, they do not find even this time suitable for establishing a locomotive workshop forthwith.' When told it was difficult getting material from England he said, 'I have some personal knowledge how Government have been able to import from America certain heavy machinery for the manufacture of munitions' and questioned 'Why did not Government in the past look ahead and establish works for manufacturing such and other spare parts of machinery? ... Whenever Government want to do a thing, they do it; when they do not want to do so, they make all sorts of excuses.'

This attitude of the Government he felt, would "strangle the development of commerce and industry ...the Minister of Transport assured the Members of the House of Commons (in England) that the Government would not use control of the railways to impose higher charges on the public' and 'clearly announced that charges would be increased only on account of increased wages and price of materials or on account of any serious difficulties due to war conditions'... with...' an emphatic assurance that such increase would have to be justified to Parliament'... he added 'Let us now look at the picture in India. I cannot understand why the British policy in England in this respect differs from that of the British policy in India".

Later he welcomed 'the intention of the Government to start making locomotives in India,' but added his 'experience in the past has been that sometimes such reports which are very rosy and when the time comes for action we find that they are shelved for good'...'the impression...is that the Government does not really want to advance the industries in India and whenever an opportunity arises measures are taken to discourage them.'

He made an important point saying that 'the deficit of ₹2 crores a year which the Indian Railways bear as an item of loss in strategic lines' should be met by the Army Department. Speaking at length of the need of not sharing such funds, 'I do not say that the military expenditure should not be met. Let it be met, but let it be met from Army funds and not from other funds." He felt that the loss on strategic railways should be debited to the Defence Department, because... all the defence expenditure ought to be consolidated.'

Against the proposal to abolish the Lower Gazetted Service of Railways he asked if this step indicated promotion of a certain percentage of the officers to superior service? Lower Gazetted Services were especially introduced in 1931 as an incentive for deserving subordinates. i.e. having good, energetic and loyal service? He asked whether the subordinates would be promoted to a superior service straight away and in what proportion and questioned how the interest of the subordinates would be safe guarded.

Speaking of discrimination he said, 'We have seen in railway travelling to what extent colour prejudice goes. We know what humiliations Indians have to face in railway travel. The sooner these conditions are improved, the better, because during the war contentment of the people is of paramount importance.'

Standing up for the rights of Indians he said, 'with several foremen being imported from Britain...Indians who were then officiating as foremen... were going to be put back' This he claimed was not Indianization, particularly as 'the prospects of Indians who came from various mechanical engineering colleges and were acting as foremen were being put at a discount.' He added, 'that on the Maclagan Engineering

College at Lahore, the majority of the Committee are officers of the N.W.R. and in case they are not able to produce capable young men, it is really the railway officers concerned who are to blame.'

He pointed out that 'As regards... the senior grade drivers, there is not a single Indian in the Howrah Division on E.I.R. There is an anomaly that Anglo-Indians are treated as Indians and that is confusing...Anglo-Indians sometimes claim themselves to be Europeans when they want to have their advantages, and they become Indians when it so suits them. That dubious position ought to be removed.'

He also questioned the rights and privileges of retired railway servants and felt some consideration should be shown to them in the matter of the employment of their sons in the railways.

COAL SHORTAGE

In the early 1920's, he voiced concern for 'there is reason to believe that the demand for coal in the country has increased more rapidly than the capacity of the railways to convey coal from the coalfields,' and enquired what steps the government... proposed to take to deal with the issue? He strongly felt that freight on coal and fuel should not be increased. Instead the higher cost could be met by increasing freight on such goods as are not significant for the industrial development of the country. He regretted the great hardship caused to traders and merchants by sudden stoppages of goods booking at short notice.

Much later in the 1940's, regarding post war measures, he was critical that industrial concerns engaged in war work were not being treated well by the Government. Inferior coal was supplied to them while one third of the first rate coal went to Ceylon, Middle East and other countries amounting to 'a step motherly treatment.' As coal was being 'utilized for non-Indian purposes and for non- industrial purposes' the Indian industry was suffering.....'The industrial concerns ... situated at long distances from coalfields have been in a very bad plight. The coal which they got was third class coal which could not burn' resulting in many concerns closing down... .'The Government of India, I understand, have pooled their resources of coal with the United Kingdom and the result is that we are getting coal which is no good to us.'

FOREIGN POLICY

A hundred years ago, as early as 1921, Ram Saran Das articulated in the inaugural session his views on what we today call the Look East or the Act East Policy. He said 'In the East, India occupies the centre of the Empire... is easily accessible to Australia in the South East, South Africa in the South West, East Africa in the West and to Persia, Mesopotamia, Palestine and Egypt in the North West. The Indian Ocean is now a British lake and India occupies a very prominent position in this lake".

In the 1930's his global interests were evident. Speaking on the Ottawa Agreement on trade and the economic situation in Europe and America, he believed that the world currency should have a fixed ratio to the sterling.

Again, when India was compared with Russia he said, 'India should not be compared with other countries which are highly industrialised...Russia is a highly industrialized country now, because their five year plans have proved great successes.'

In the 1940's he candidly expressed his views on the situation in South Africa, "Sir, I am one of those who believe that ungratefulness is the biggest sin that one can commit and that applies in the case of the Union Government. Everyone knows that Africa was conquered by the Indians and before the conquest the Boer, who were the enemies of the British, were then fighting against Britain. The Proclamation of Her late Majesty Queen Victoria lays down that there should not be any distinction between the various classes and creeds of subjects, but I find that in Africa the Union Government has been violating this pledge. General Smuts does not like that any South African should be put under the command of an Indian. If my information is correct, General Smuts fell out with our popular Commander-in-Chief, His Excellency Sir Claude Auchinleck, because Sir Claude appointed an Indian Brigadier and General Smuts took strong exception to Africans being put under command of an Indian and pressed and prevailed upon Mr. Churchill for removal of His Excellency from the Command'....'the self-respect of India is fast reviving and they cannot stand any nonsense of this kind....When such things happen trade and diplomatic relations are cut off. My own feeling is that when such like circumstances exist there must be a complete boycott of the South Africans who are serving in India in any capacity....We are talking about the principle and not about personalities. Indians should refuse to work under any African...The Union Government has been most ungrateful to Indians who have developed the country, who have made it what it is now... Indian troops now stationed in South Africa should be immediately withdrawn. We do not want to help those who hate Indians...Let the Africans fight for themselves. We are not going to shed the blood of our people for those who hate us and have no regard for us'...' I strongly feel that the Government of India should break off its diplomatic ties and trade relations with the Union

Government. I do not want to blame anybody but my own conscience says that the British Government has not helped us to the extent, that it ought to have done. My own impression is that as long as Mr. Churchill is the British Premier India will get nothing. Even the present reforms were strongly opposed by Mr. Churchill. .. platitudes that the Indian Army has done very well do not mean anything. They have shed their blood for their King and country but we find no reward in practice....I do not think that our High Commissioner should remain there any longer and be humiliated and slighted... When Indian troops have done so well to serve their King and country and when testimony is given even by Right Honourable Mr Churchill—I do not know whether he meant it really or simply politically because politics are a game and diplomacy is a privilege.'

A passage from the speech made by the Right Honourable Srinivasa Sastri was read out, making it clear that the British were the root of the problem-

'The white population in Natal was entirely British. They had put pressure on the Union Government to introduce the present legislation to protect what they considered to be the European area of the city of Durban from encroachment by the Indian population. It was, therefore, not the Afrikander but the Britisher who was at the bottom of the present troubles.'

Again in the 1940's, 'I welcome the proposals in regard to the dollar reserve. But the dollar reserve must be at the command of the Indian Government and should be spent on imports from America....Why should we not get from America the machinery and the machine parts that we want for our various industrial concerns? My information is that Americans are afraid of competition in future from India, and

January, 1929. 'Since then a number of clubs were established in India without Government financial aid' which 'did solid work' as 'at the outbreak of the war they were able to provide a great number of pilots. The object of establishing these flying clubs was to make the Indians air-minded and on that ground Government accepted that policy and introduced subsidies.' He felt 'the Air Force is the chief arm of defence and that there is a great paucity of pilots...Members had been always advocating that in the Indian defence forces there ought to be a sufficient number of commissioned Indian officers and that Indianisation should go on at its promised pace.' Critical of the present stance he questioned why the 'Government have to go to places like Australia, Canada and South Africa to find air pilots for their force.' He brought to notice that in the Indian flying clubs training extended to 75 flying hours, but in contrast 'training by the Defence Department had been reduced to 25 hours which made the pilots not up to the mark and below the general standard prescribed by other countries.' He wanted that clubs should continue receiving subsidies lamenting that even in the institutions founded by the Defence Department boys were not trained on the modern aircrafts.

Crucial questions were asked regarding the number of squadrons in the Indian Air Force and how many had King's Indian commissioned officers as commanding officers ad adjutants and how many of these had been appointed as wing commanders.

EDUCATION

As early as 1921, Ram Saran Das laid emphasis on the role of education. As 80% of the population in India was dependent on agriculture it was an established practice that boys helped during the sowing, weeding and harvesting season. Thus the average duration of school life was restricted to 4 years, commencing at the age of 5 or 6 with completion by the age of 9 or 10. He strongly recommended that between the ages of 9 and 12, boys should not be allowed to work in factories. Instead free compulsory education should be provided during those crucial years.

His queries on education were not restricted to Punjab alone and in 1932 expressed concern regarding boarding houses of the Government High School in Delhi. He raised a Resolution in the Council to guarantee a certain fixed number of appointments every year in the Mechanical and other departments of State Railways for qualified students of Maclagam Engineering College, Lahore and similar colleges in other Provinces of India.

In the 1940's he expressed unhappiness. 'I have been during the 29 years of my life in the Legislatures always pointing out to the Government the defect in the present system of education. I generally describe the present education as Godless. The products of the universities and schools are not what similar products in other civilized countries are. Therefore many Indians send their boys to England, to Cambridge, to Oxford and other Universities for education rather than educate them in India. Ever since the portfolio of Education was established in the Government of India, the value of real education has considerably gone down.'

INDUSTRY

A nationalist to the core, Ram Saran Das enquired in the 1930's what measures were being taken to prevent foreign governments from exploiting the Indian market. Worried that the Japanese industry would capture Indian cotton and sugar markets by not allowing them to flourish on account of heavy dumping, he believed that anti-dumping measures were essential. He was concerned that the Japanese underselling goods such as paint, cement, sugar candy, cotton, woollen, cotton and woollen hosiery would affect Indian markets and industries negatively. In the General Budget Debate he said that though the imposed duty on artificial silk goods had been raised from 17% to 27%, the factual position was that the Japanese exchange had gone down so low as to nullify the good effect of this extra taxation.

He regretted that 'no serious consideration had really been given to the protection of many important industries in India".

When informed that the freight war between the indigenous Indian shipping companies and foreign companies was still under consideration, he questioned if the Government was waiting till the present indigenous companies were forced to liquidate?

Looking futuristically, he spoke about five year programmes. 'Many countries, particularly Russia, have set out a 5 year programme and by that programme the country has very materially progressed", suggesting that there should be a similar programme for planning in respect of agriculture and industry.

In the 1940's he enquired why the Government had placed orders for shipping vessels in Mexico, 'a country which was not an Empire country, though they have not seen their way to subsidize the shipping industry in India.' He felt 'the automobile industry for the construction of motor cars' could easily be associated with the aeroplane industry.' This would be possible only if the Government gave 'some sort of patronage by placing orders for certain number of military lorries,' thereby resulting in the company flourishing and India becoming self contained as far as the automobile industry was concerned. 'Certain industries, for instance, the cotton textile industry, have been suffering for the last many years from the keen competition of other countries and particularly from Japan.

'As regards the manufacture of the various parts of aeroplanes...a regular survey of the possibilities was made by the Chief Inspector of Aircraft. There was at that time no suitable steel being made in this country. That is a thing that we think can be overcome. Tatas are confident that they could with sufficient demand make a steel which would be suitable for the purpose....Here the Government is trying to raise as much money as it can for the war and therefore if a private company comes forward and undertakes the work, Government ought to welcome and patronize it....My own view is that the Government in the last few years did not think it proper to patronize or to establish this industry, which according to my information, has been under consideration of the company since 1936. If they had done this and patronized the company set up, India would not have now to face the difficulty in finding chassis and other stores for the Supply Department.'

'Why should Australia,' he asked, 'a country which is too far away from most of the British Colonies and Dominions be given preferential treatment by subsidizing them in establishing shipbuilding. Why should not similar assistance be given to Indian shipbuilding?'... 'As regards shipping I said that shipbuilding yards should be encouraged. ...When the British Government is getting their shipping orders booked in Mexico and the United States, a reasonable number of ships should be placed at the service of India to meet its requirements.'

Regarding the plight of the sugar industry he said 'there has been a restriction to the export of sugar, while on the other hand His Majesty's Government has agreed to purchase the entire exportable sugar crop of Australia, the Union of South Africa. Mauritius. Fiji and British West Indies....Why is this differential treatment in the case of India?' The Dutch East Indies he had been told were to be given big concessions as regards of import of sugar to India.

He saw 'the apathy of the Government... in imposing an excise duty on rubber tyres and tubes' and added that 'This industry was established in Calcutta mainly by the Dunlop Rubber Company and the Goodyear Rubber Company. The intention of the promoters of these two companies was that Indian labour be employed and that import duty be avoided.'.... They are encouraging the industry only by platitudes and not in practice.'

INDIAN INTEREST

Regarding bungalows being acquired in the Peshawar Cantonment in the 1930's, Ram Saran Das said, "Is it a fact that not a single bungalow occupied by a Non-Military European or Anglo-Indian is intended to be acquired and that only Indian residents of such bungalows will be affected by this acquisition proceedings?" He informed them that there were 'large areas available within the limits of Peshawar Cantonment, in which bungalows can be built, including three Polo Grounds.'

MILITARY EXPENDITURE

In the 1940's, while lauding India's support to Britain in the war effort, Ram Saran Das was unhappy in the manner it was being done. He said,'...the practice hitherto had been of presenting the details of military to the Central Legislative Assembly but now the estimates are presented in a lump sum and the Assembly is not being given a chance to discuss the details of the military expenditure.' This was resented by the people and he felt that 'the Government would be well advised to appoint an Indian Committee or Member of the Executive Council to see to policy and the details of the military expenditure.'

He questioned the cost of the war, measures, the Indian liability and lump sum payment of ₹1 crore towards the extra costs of maintaining India's External Defence Troops overseas. He reproachfully added, 'this is a matter, which, along with India being dragged into the war without consultation with even its foremost leaders, has created a sort of discontent and I strongly advise the Government to appraise the feelings of the people by a timely gesture.'

He questioned why war expenditure in India was not fully or even partly met by war loans and brought to notice a press report stating that the British Government was floating a sterling loan of pounds 300 millions. 'When a rich country like England takes that step, why should not India follow that course? The present economic condition of the Indians is at a very low ebb and India cannot conveniently bear the burden... I want peace in the country and there should be only so much taxation as is absolutely necessary for carrying on the Government in war time.' He requested the Honourable Finance Minister 'to reconsider his proposals and to float a war loan to meet the present deficit of about ₹8 crores odd and not burden the country with any further taxation at a time which they are just recovering from the economic depression into which they had been put'.

Opposing military expenditure he said 'no justification has been made to prove the necessity for meeting this enormously heavy expenditure;...The percentage of army expenditure to our income is unparallel and 'from the figures which I have studied I find that no country in the world bears such a big expenditure in the army as compared to their income'.

He enquired whether 'the amount promised by the British Government as Defence contribution had yet been paid and asked the 'Government to lay on the Table of the House a statement showing the scales of salaries and allowances of members of the Consular Services (a) Indians and (b) Europeans' and whether there was a difference in the scales and if so would the Government give reasons for such differences..

He continued, 'Our experience in the appropriation of the last Great War accounts showed that there was not a satisfactory apportionment of the war expenditure between the War Office and the Indian Government. All expenditures incurred abroad which did not exceed ₹50,000 was debitable to the Indian Government and bigger amounts were debitable to the War Office. Our information then was that big sums were split up into parcels of ₹50,000 and were thus debited to the Government of India'.

He further asked for clarification as regards borders saying, '...we do not know where our Defence borders are and where the Indian Government's responsibility ends and that of the War Office begins....Does our Defence expenditure extend to Egypt or Benghazi or to Morocco or Shanghai and

Singapore or where?

With the Government enforcing compulsory war insurance, he proposed that the income of the war insurance should be kept separate and utilized for the benefit of industry and not be allowed to merge in the general revenue of the country. He felt as far as the general public was concerned, the Reserve Bank ought to be allowed to play a great part in the financial policy of the Government and its Directorate ought to be consulted.

TAXATION

Ram Saran Das was against the heavy taxation imposed on people during the war years of the 1940's saying though the Government insists they are not taxing the agriculturists, according to his information, 'over ₹325 crores of gold has gone out of India and it is because the agriculturist has no means to support himself.'.....'The condition of business has been one of constant economic depression, and just when the agriculturists and the industrialist are recovering from that unprecedented period of depression the Government wants to share the profits.' Why should business men, he felt, be put to such taxation as their income varies from year to year? 'Why should not those people, who have a permanent income, share the burdens of war.'

He strongly felt that as expenditure declared by the Finance Minister had gone up to 45 crores, this should only be partially met by taxation from the people as the Indians cannot bear such a burden. India, he said, could not be compared to Britain where the average income per person was ₹1800 a year as against the yearly income of ₹80 of an Indian. 'We all wish that the war should be won and we are prepared to make sacrifices for it, but there is a limit to that sacrifice'. The repatriation of the sterling debt would result in deflation and he understood that the Directors of the Reserve Bank had not been consulted.

He sought clarification regarding the following Bill due to be passed—

'That the Bill to impose on employers a liability to pay compensation to workmen sustaining war injuries and to provide to the insurance of employees against such liability as passed by the Legislative Assembly be taken into consideration.'

He asked. '...whether the premium thus paid will be deducted from income-tax while assessing income-tax. Employers of labour ...are paying a very heavy taxation and I should like the point to be cleared'

He felt that 'under estimation of revenues has become rather a vice with the Finance Department. Every year the income is under-estimated and taxes are levied and then at the end of the year there is a surplus and no relief given to the taxpayer. I call this Budget a fleecing Budget because ....the Finance Minister is trying to fleece out the people of India by heavily increasing taxation every year without regard to their ability to pay......Government should see that the people of India are not totally depleted of their scanty savings if any'.

PRICE CONTROL

In the 1940's, not in favour of price control, Ram Saran Das said, 'We in India, live mostly on agriculture and in case the agriculturist or the landholder prospers, every other industry and commerce will prosper. It is in the interests of India to let the people recover from the grave economic depression that they experienced during the last 10 years. To regulate and control the prices now at a lower level will not certainly be in the interests of India.'

'There is another point which as a commercial man I want to put before the House. I want information from the Government of India as regards stocks which each province ought to have for times of emergency. If the entire stocks are cleared every year, what will you do when there is an emergency of India becoming a centre of warfare? It has also been observed that we should not depend upon imports of foodstuffs from other countries. ...as far as wheat is concerned, India consumes about 9 ½ million tons and whenever the yield of the rabi crop is over 9 ½ tons the necessity of export arises As far as the regulation of prices is concerned, I can say that the rise in prices has been due to the wrong measures adopted by various Government agencies.....I know that in certain markets these agents broke the control rate themselves and purchased foodstuffs at much higher prices and if I am not wrong, the purchases were made in such a way that three middlemen were appointed in the same firm; one was buying from another and the last one sold it to the Government purchase agents at enhanced prices.' He said 'the present way of price control and the present system of purchase will never succeed.'

He suggested that 'in order to control or regulate prices of foodstuff, Government should take revenue in cash and in kind and the commodity that they take in kind ought to be kept as a reserve against the prices going up. They must throw the reserve into the market to bring down the prices if necessary. His second suggestion was 'that they must get moral sanction from the leaders. Government Ordinances will not carry weight--- they will be un-effective unless they are supported by the moral sanction of recognised Indian leaders.

He suggested that 'the only right way now controlling the foodstuffs is to buy the whole crop. Have a Committee of public men as well as officials to advise in the matter' of distribution of the whole stock. 'Rationing in so many cities... will be dispensed with then because when you have the public co-operating, these things can be cheaply managed with a small staff than with a big staff'.

HINDU TRADITIONS

As early as 1921 he raised the subject of Hindu Dharamshastras saying, "It cannot be denied that during the long years that British courts have been working, Hindu law has been to some extent modified by case law. In my opinion, however, this should not have been the case".

Later in the 1940's he was of the opinion that "Legislative measures which affect any particular community ought to have the consent of that community before the introduction of that legislative measure. I would like the same clause embodied in our constitution to safeguard the interests of the minority communities and particularly those who belong to the orthodox classes.

As regards amendment in the Hindu law he said,"...being connected with one of the orthodox provincial institutions in the Punjab I must say that it is only when the reformers can carry the masses with them that their utterances in the Legislature will have effect'...

BENGAL FAMINE

Ram Saran Das criticized the handling of the possibility of a Japanese invasion in Bengal in 1942. '...thousands of boats were taken over by the Bengal Government. Many villages were evacuated and people were deprived of their livelihood and habitations without finding for them any suitable substitute. In England, my information is that when any area is to be vacated, the civil authorities must house the people affected and all facilities are given to them. ...In the other House an observation was made that some of these boats have been returned to the people....but I can say that the condition of these boats is so bad that they will not be workable. The fear of Japanese invasion began in April-May 1942 and certain areas were placed under military control and all those people who were made to vacate were not provided with any accommodation in other parts of Bengal.'

Another aspect he raised was in regard to the supply of rice to Bengal from Burma. "I want to ask the Government of India and the Government of Bengal why they were sleeping'... Burma has been in the possession of Japan for more than a year. My information is that a million and a half tons of rice used to come from Burma and the Bengal Government knew that this supply had been cut off by the occupation of Burma. Notwithstanding the fact that the province was short of a million and a half tons of rice, the Bengal Government allowed the export of rice to other countries....notwithstanding the fact that Assam and Bengal were probably to be the future field of warfare". In response to a statement made by a Punjab Minister he said, 'Bengal requires rice. Bengal is not a wheat eating province and I cannot understand what is meant by all this propaganda of the Minister of the Punjab Government saying that they had so much spare wheat and that the Government of India failed transport it'.....There must be some reserve stocks with the people to meet emergencies and they ought not to be deprived of even the small stock they have.'

As regards expenditure on the Burma Campaign he questioned. 'Will Government state whether the Government of India, at the instance of the Secretary of State, is bearing all expenses in connection with the reconquest of Burma?

As regards the food situation in Bengal he said, "I judge people by their actions and the results that they achieve thereby and not by pure propaganda and talk. The Government of India ...realising that there was to be a shortage of food grains owing to the influx of troops from abroad and other reasons, ordered 2 ½ lakh tons of foodgrains from England...about a lakh of tons of foodgrain arrived at Karachi. Later on, when the Food Department was created, further shipments were stopped. I want to know from the Government Member in charge why further consignments were stopped and by whom. My information is that some responsible official of the Bengal Government...said that there were plenty of foodgrains in Bengal and nothing further was needed. The spokesman of the Government said that Bengal will be 'flooded' with foodstuffs. As a consequence of such statements, perhaps the import of the rest of the food grains was stopped. The result was that the shipping that was arranged by the British Government was diverted to South Africa....in case the rest of the consignments had arrived in India the situation would not have worsened to such an extent.

I wanted to go myself to Bengal and offer my personal services to my suffering countrymen, but the state of my health would not permit me to do so. However, the Sanatan Dharam Pratinidhi Sabha, of which I have the privilege to be the President, sent a relief party of 150 persons and proposed to send 50 railway wagon loads of foodgrains. My information from our workers and other sources is that things were being so badly managed that people had lost confidence in the

Government which resulted in the present condition of misery and distress.'

A government official shook his head indicating dissent, on hearing criticism of Government handling of the famine. This provoked him to retort, "You may shake your head but I know it is a fact". He regretted that the Government had "not availed themselves of the co-operation of public leaders, particularly Mahatma Gandhi" and criticised the purchase system of not having minimum emergency stocks of foodstuff and its failure to prevent hoarding as encouraged by a Minister. He added," Provincial Governments have provincial autonomy. But in such matters they should not go against the Government of India and encourage people to hoard stocks... Is there a clique in which the Government of India is a party? Why has that challenge not been met by the Government of India? That particular Minister advised the people to hoard stocks of foodstuff in order to get better prices". He concluded, "With these words, Sir, I express the hope that the Government will associate Mahatma Gandhi and other public leaders with them and with their co-operation successfully achieve the end they have in view". He was also very critical of the export of rice before the Bengal famine and said, "My own view is that the Government of India and the Government of Bengal have failed in their prime duty of protecting the people from starvation.'

MAHATMA GANDHI

In 1944, the last session he attended before his death there were different references to Mahatma Gandhi. Again intervening in a debate when there was a reference by Sir Jwala Prasad Srivastava and others to associate the public with the work of the Food Department he just added two words,' including Mahatma Gandhi.' Srivastave responded, "Yes, most welcome, if he comes along, Sir".

He asked pointedly on March 29, 1944 "whether Mahatma Gandhi asked Government to permit the eminent Ayurvedic physician Pandit Shiv Sharma to take up the treatment of Mrs Kasturba Gandhi, if so on what date and how many days after the requisition was Pandit Sharma allowed contact with the patient?" The Government response was that the first definite request for Pandit Sharma's services was made to the Government of India on February 9, and was granted on Feb 10. It appears that there must have been some delay for this question to be asked because Kasturba Gandhi died on Feb 22, 44. The reply was not straightforward as the Government response used the word 'definite'.

CONGRESS

Regarding the deadlock between the Government and the Congress in 1942, Ram Saran Das said, "the present agitation of the Congress differs very much from the agitation which it previously carried on. The Premiers and the Ministers regarding whom the Government of India and the British Government had at times paid high tribute are now confined in jail. What are those people? They are the real representatives of the public. They have a large following and by confining them in jail I do not know what advantage the Government is getting......Generally speaking the people of India are not content for some reason or another and the Government should in their own interest and in the interests of India find out a solution".

With prevalent unrest he said that' there was a fundamental

difference of outlook between the Government and this side of the House regarding the origin of the disturbances and the requirements of the situation. The reason for this diversity is that the Government is to my mind suffering from propaganda complex. Having made up its mind not to part with power, it realised that it must one day come into clash with the Congress. It prepared itself for that clash in the convenient belief that the Congress could be crushed at a stroke.... Having assumed that the Congress movement would have no backing, it gave to the world a daily picture of "All quiet on all fronts". For some weeks, we were told that there were hardly any disturbances worth mentioning and the All India Radio even ceased mentioning the matter after the first few days....Suddenly the Government appears to have changed its propaganda angle. It has now let loose an account of arson, loot, murder and sabotage to show that it had been faced with "an open rebellion" and that but for the loyalty of the military, the police and the Government servants the rebellion might have paralysed the machinery of the Government. At the same time we are given the assurance that the general public has remained steady and has not supported the rebels. What can be the motive of publishing now these blood-curdling accounts of hooliganism? I suspect that the motive is to keep the Congress leaders locked up in jail for the period of the war and to carry on the administration on the existing patterns.

The refusal to allow Dr. Mukerjee to see Mahatma Gandhi is a pointer in the same direction...I am not here to plead for the Congress. I have all my life had differences with the Congress programme and I unreservedly condemn the outburst of violence which followed the arrest of Congress leaders. But what I wish to know is whether the Government feels satisfied that after imprisoning the Congress leaders it has done its job and that it can take a complacent view of the situation of the country"'.

He adds 'I have a stake in the country and during my long public life I have been a supporter of ordered progress. I am pained to find today that the Government stands friendless. Even those classes... who were Government's most loyal supporters are not without misgivings as to the policy Government is pursuing...They are only out to promote their narrow interests. At a time like this when public opinion is becoming more and more divorced from Government it is the path of wisdom to adopt the policy of conciliation.'

'No one denies that that there has been mob violence and that the Government has done well by putting it down at once, but the whole basis of Government and the psychology of its agents convert the instrument of force into a weapon of repression. It is the lesson of history that extreme repression leads to extreme reaction. I have no hesitation saying that that the Defence of India Act is being misused"....'Both Mr, Churchill and Mr. Amery have made the situation worse by their utterances. I wish they had not spoken, but now, since they have, it is up to the Government of India to convey to them the true reaction in India to those speeches....you have completely misjudged the situation and that you will continue to do so at your peril. The Congress Party which held the reins of Government in seven provinces is not so unimportant as you wish to make out. But conceding that it has put itself out of court by making the demand for "Quit India" why not transfer power to those who represent the steady public opinion which you say is behind the war effort? There never was a time when this country was governed more autocratically than today.... in a number of districts in Bihar...confidence in the (Indian) I.C.S officers according to my information has been lost.

Collective fines are being imposed without discrimination. There are people who have done nothing and even they are to pay fines. It is alleged properties were burnt by police.

JINNAH AND THE MUSLIM LEAGUE

Reference in the 1940's to 'this new theme of Pakistan Empire' being developed 'which I consider to be not in the interests of India' shows that Ram Saran Das was against the concept of partition.

He also expressed concern, "In Lahore at times a few hundred people armed with swords or lances, etc. march into the city crying all sorts of slogans and such marches were a source of great danger to peace and order". He was against organisations which had a political motive behind or whose activities have resulted in the breach of peace and order"

Regarding the Muslims wanting a separate state and being in indifferent health he said, 'I had no mind to speak on the Finance Bill owing to my present state of health, but I want to make only a few observations which have been necessitated by the remarks of some of my Honourable Muslim friends. This is a time when no useful purpose can be served by raising communal issues or by Muslims regarding themselves as a separate nation'..I am advocating universal brotherhood. Even with some sacrifices, with a good will mission, we ought to promote brotherly feelings and not take any steps which might widen the gulf between the Hindus and Musalmans. I simply want to tell the House that 98 per cent Musalmans are converts from Hinduism. There is only a very small percentage of 2 per cent Musalmans who migrated into India from other countries".

Bringing to notice the role played by the British

Government in helping Jinnah to acquire a house in Lahore, he asked, "Will the Government state whether it is a fact that a bungalow on the Davies Road Lahore, now occupied by military personnel, which has been purchased for Mr. Jinnah is being vacated by the military authorities for his residence? The response of the Commander in Chief was vague, stating that he has not been able to verify the facts because the exact location of the bungalow had not been given. That the Government was evading the issue, was obvious.

When a member expressing his point of view stated that people in Bengal are starving and dying out of spite for the Muslim League, he responded saying he found this statement "very surprising". ..."no man will die for any such spite against the Muslim League Ministry. My information, from my workers and my friends in Bengal is that the non-Muslims have completely lost the confidence in the Muslim League Government and wanted that the work of distribution of money and food-grains should be entrusted to certain recognized institutions or reliable parties to be appointed for that purpose. Sir, the President of the Muslim League set a very bad example in earmarking his charity for Muslims alone. Naturally, the Muslim League Government has to follow the policy of its President. This policy is also responsible for depriving the non-Muslims of their legitimate share in the public charity. My information is that the Chamber through which the Muslim League was working opened their free joint kitchens and langars both to Hindus and Muslims. In an orthodox Province like Bengal it was quite evident that no non-Muslim will take any food from such kitchens. So, the point that those langars were meant for all communities is misleading.....In Bengal, when there is no warfare going on if that is the condition of the people, what will be their fate if it becomes a country of war. No Government can be proud of so many of its subjects dying of starvation".

CONCERN FOR INDIAN SOLDIERS

In the early 1940's in reference to the Indian soldiers Ram Saran Das said, "I am proud that our Indian regiments have been able to capture Kerren and Harrar. I offer congratulations to them and also convey my admiration for the traditional bravery of the Indian troops engaged in Africa who have contributed to the decisive victory which the Imperial forces have secured over the Italians...my information is that during the Boer War Indians were mainly responsible for the victory in East Africa".

He recommended the establishment of an Advisory Defence Council where chosen Indian leaders should have a voice in the expenditure of Defence services and advocated, 'more the taxation, more the representation.' He felt racial discrimination existed as regards salaries and allowances of the superior Defence services. Indian officers, he felt incurred more expenditure than European officers, as they had to entertain both European and Indian officers in addition to supporting their near and distant relatives, and give presents for the many festivals. The Europeans, in contrast, had no extra expenditure apart from what they spent on their wife and children.

No European regiment, he stated, had been stationed at the Frontier. Due to extremes of climate, he insisted the best material to withstand this should be provided to soldiers who were based there and 'the people in fighting units must be those who can well stand such extremes.'

"The differential treatment accorded to Anglo-Indians as compared to Indians is resented by the public. I find that certain Anglo-Indians who are not normally eligible for appointment in the army or entitled to certain allowances are allowed those advantages but in the case of Indians in the same grade and in the same place...they are refused. In times of war it is not wise for the Government to create that sort of differentiation, because that creates heart burning."

"Another point which is agitating the Indian mind is the difference in pay and allowances between the British and Indian commissioned officers. We all admit that overseas allowance should be given to British officers, but as regards other allowances, both Europeans and Indians should be at par. There must be no discrimination of any sort'.....'the position of the officers joining from the Indian Sandhurst, Dehra Dun, should be improved. They should not be dignified jamadars. They must start their life as company officers and not as platoon commanders'...'in the Defence Services ...all sorts of people are being given King's commissions in the British recruitment—tea planters, lorry drivers and what not. They are being given King's commission freely. But in the case of Indians, different rules are being observed."

Drawing attention to the Indians in the Defence forces he said, "I am one of those who are of opinion that the present war should be won and that causes of discontent should be removed. He said,...'recommendations of the Skeen Committee as far as Indianization is concerned, which were accepted by the Government of India, were not translated into practise... This led Indians to think that the policy of the Government in pace of Indianization has been reversed. Another point which has created discontent among Indians was the creation of the Indianized units...segregation was the result of discrimination and hatred... In the Skeen Committee Report, it is mentioned that there was a fall in numbers of British officers for service in India as they disliked serving under Indians in various Government defence services, but a responsible official assured Britishers that in the defence services they would not be put under the command of a blackie. That impression still continues because the pace of Indianisation instead of improving is getting worse.' He added, 'for the sake of the increased war effort there should be no discontent... on account of racial discrimination and consequential segregation in Government services. I want Indians to be allowed to enter all units; there should be encouragement of comradeship and brotherhood amongst all officers.'

He asked the Government to "lay on the table of this House a comparative statement showing the salaries and allowances payable to British commissioned officers and other personnel of various defence units and those payable to Indian commissioned officers and other personnel.

He wanted to know had "the attention of the Government of India been drawn to the statement of the Right Honourable Mr. Churchill regarding the increase of salaries and allowances of British commissioned officers and personnel serving in the defence units? Do these increases also apply to the Indian commissioned officers and personnel or not?

Commenting on the statement made by General Hartley that the proportion of Indian officers to British officers in Defence Units was 4.75 British officers to one Indian, he said, "The salaries and allowances of the British King's commissioned officers are different from those of the Indian commissioned officers and racial discrimination still exists in the Navy, in the Air Force and in the land forces... When

Indians can do quite as well as the British officers why should there be increased recruitment of British officers?"

Standing up for the rights and raising the plight of those serving in the war he said, "I had occasion to meet many officers who have come from the war theatres and...they all think that when their legitimate demands are not met during the war they have absolutely no hope of their being met in the near future... It is religion which prompts everyone to serve his King and country. I have no faith in the loyalty of those who ignore religion.....Even now the majority of people serving in the army do not want food which their religion prohibits. If you ask any Muslim, Sikh or Hindu to take prohibited food, he will never agree...I would, therefore, strongly request His Excellency Sir Claude Auchinleck to expedite this decision and to avoid the grouse of Indian officers and men who are shedding their blood in the field and meet their legitimate grievances. The view.. is that if this legitimate demand is not met now, it will never be met."

He queried, "'whether any Indian Air Force training class has been opened at Aligarh,' and 'when does the Government intend to open similar classes at the Hindu University, Benaras, and at the Khalsa College, Amritsar?'" The answer to the first was affirmed but training in four other universities was being considered.

He said, "I think that at this time when the British Prime Minister and other responsible statesmen in Britain have paid a tribute to the services of the Indian troops, it behoves the British Government not to evade the issue but to intervene in the matter and get Indians the rights which they legitimately are entitled to or give constitutional power to India to retaliate in the manner it likes. The question of franchise is a very important one and even the rights which the Indians hitherto enjoyed are being taken away from them. At this time, the co-operation of all those countries which are helping the Allies is a very important factor. The question of colour and creed should vanish and the rights of Indians overseas should be respected by the Colonial as well as the Dominion Governments. It has been acknowledged by the authorities that the Japanese and Russians are showing the right spirit in this field.'

He demanded that 'the Government lay before the House a statement showing the following: a) The pay, allowances, and other facilities admissible to the Indian Military personnel combatants, the payments, allowances and other facilities enjoyed by the British and other non-Indian personnel of His Majesty's armed forces in India, when serving in India and when in active service ex-India.

b) The payments, allowances and other facilities enjoyed by the personnel of the British, Colonial and Dominions troops when on active service in the various theatres of war and also the pays, allowances and other facilities granted to the Indian officers and soldiers serving in the same theatres of war and under like conditions."

Referring to the revision of scales of pay and allowances in the British army and Indian army he asked, "Will the Government lay a statement on the table showing the extent of the revision of the scales of pays and allowances of and the grant of fresh allowances to the personnel of Britain's fighting forces, sanctioned by His Majesty's Government since the outbreak of the Great War of 1914-18, and also the extent of the revision of the scales of pays and allowances of—

i) The Indian personnel
ii) The non-Indian personnel of His Majesty's armed

forces in India sanctioned by the Government of India during the same period.

On a suggestion that Indian troops who are serving abroad should be brought back to India, he questioned 'Why should India be burdened with troops whose maintenance costs three or four times as much as the maintenance of Indian troops? Some people think that the Government has lost confidence in Indians and therefore they are keeping Europeans, Colonial and American troops in India. In India, the self-respect of Indians having revived, they cannot now stand any racial discrimination and humiliation. I understand that in Assam, Indian troops , except excepting Gurkhas are kept back from the field areas between Burma and Assam. If that is a fact, that also proves the want of confidence on the part of the Government of India."

CONCERN FOR INDIANS ABROAD

Coming to the difficulties faced by Indians overseas in the 1940's, Ram Saran Das said, "In Burma, Ceylon and in Indo-China, Indians have been put to great inconvenience. ....I know that our Honourable Member for Emigration is doing all he can, but after all there are certain limitations, and unless the Government in England takes interest in the matter, much cannot be achieved".

Regarding the plight of the Indians in Trinidad and British Guiana he questioned 'the religious disabilities to which Hindus particularly are being subjected in Trinidad and British Guiana. Representatives from Indians reached the Punjab Provincial Sanatan Dharma Pratinidhi Sabha of which I am privileged to be the President, asking us to do something for the people there who were in great difficulties...One of the difficulties was that unless the marriage of Hindus was registered their progeny was considered illegitimate.' Also they could not avail of the educational, civic and other sanitary facilities as these were not affordable....Public impression is that the promises of the Indian Government seldom materialise as far as the Colonial Office and the Foreign Office are concerned.'

AGRICULTURE

Concerned about the agricultural workers and after a debate on a Resolution **(March 1933)** Ram Saran Das asked "what has happened in Punjab? The money lending class which used to lend money before are fast disappearing and a money lending class out of the agricultural classes themselves has arisen which is charging extortionist rates of interest.' He wanted measures taken to protect the agricultural workers and money lenders to be replaced by an institution by which agriculturalists could get money at cheaper rates of interest. This suggestion was widely cheered in the House.

Regarding the 'Grow More Food Campaign' in the 1940's he felt it was merely propaganda. He questioned what facilities the Provincial Governments had offered to encourage this Grow More Food policy, adding, "In case anybody finds it a paying concern he will take to it himself' but felt the drawback has been the shortage of agricultural implements and agricultural cattle. "Prices of such implements have run so high that people find it impossible in certain areas to grow more food. Growing more food is an economic question. If I have more land, better implements and good seeds I will certainly cultivate more lands and get more profit". To improve the output of agriculture, he suggested that the "Government should lend agricultural machinery to the various landholders for ploughing, thrashing and for other purposes connected with agriculture'" When told that some steam ploughs and machinery had been tried out but failed, he said, "it failed because the present holdings are so small that until Government finds requisite machinery and provides good manure we cannot successfully derive any benefit because the areas are too small to be dealt with by machinery".

Regarding the situation in the Punjab he said that in spite of the improved seeds and crop, land has gone down in price, because the buyers of the land have been limited by legislation. An agriculturalist has been defined as one engaged in agriculture and not one who is engaged in tilling the soil.... legislative measures have failed to give the desired relief to the tillers of the soil...unless some agency is formed to replace the old agency, no practical good can come out. Governments, by their legislative measures, have wiped out the existing agency without providing a substitute. We have been hearing for years that the Provincial Governments, through the Reserve Bank are devising methods to finance the poor agriculturalists. Banks, as they are constituted at present, naturally want some security against loans...The Government of the United Provinces some time ago, appointed a Committee to go into this question and recommend measures for an effective solution of rural indebtedness. My suggestion now, is that some practical and effective way should be found to replace the banking agency which has been wiped out by the Government without finding a substitute. Unless this is done academic discussions will be absolutely of no use.' He also cautioned that 'zamindars who are minting money, do not make use of these heavy profits in accelerating the extinction of the poor smaller land-holder".

With regards to landholders not getting advantage over

industrialists he said, "I as a land-holder know that the present high prices which we are getting for our produce are and have hitherto been unknown. I find..that like the United Kingdom Commercial Corporation certain firms in India are also being unduly patronized at the cost of the agriculturalists....in the Punjab the so-called custodians of land-holders interests in power are sleeping over the matter. The prices paid to the land-holders for their products are far less than those which, the middleman or these favoured concerns are getting. This is deplorable."

TRADE MARKS

Ram Saran Das took active part in early 1940's on discussions regarding Trademarks and lamented that "there has been a lot of unpleasantness and litigation on Trade Marks' because information in respect of them had not been sent to all Chambers of Commerce". Having had a personal experience of this he wished this to be corrected.

FLAGRANTLY BIASED TREATMENT

Standing up for the downtrodden in the 1930's Ram Saran Das expressed grief "on the treatment which those poor coolies who made all these big buildings for the Government in New Delhi have received from the Government. I find that those Public Works Department officers who did well in building up the big capital were honoured with Knighthoods and other Meritorious Orders, but those poor labourers who helped the authorities in the construction of New Delhi were recently ordered to quit the land forthwith where they lived for so many years past, so much so, that even their supply of drinking water was cut off. That is the honour that is the reward, which these poor fellows have received."He concluded by saying, "they worked hard here in building up this capital and do not deserve the harsh treatment given to these people who well deserved a reward"

He raised questions regarding payment of instalments due on the loan granted by the Government in connection with Kohat riots; the working of the postal system in Punjab and measures taken against gas attacks.

Questioning increase of rates and fares of railways during war years, he added 'the jute industry, the woollen industry and the leather industry are the only industries which have benefited by war, and it is a pity that the Government has not considered the plight of other industries.

AMENDMENT OF INDIAN COINAGE ACT

Speaking on a bill to amend the Indian Coinage Act 1906 in 1940, Ram Saran Das wondered "why the proportion of silver in the quarter rupee coin had been reduced to fifty percent and fifty per cent alloy" had been mixed. When reminded by the President of the House that valid reasons had been given for this by the Government, he sharply retorted 'those reasons are not convincing enough".

I.C.S.

Describing the I.C.S. in the 1940's as one of the gifted services with the best brains, intellect and ability...a glorious body with the very best of men, but, sadly as a result of communal representation there had been a lowering in efficiency. Communal representation, Ram Saran Das felt, would work well provided equally capable and efficient men were recruited and selection made from among those who appeared in a competitive exam. He added that "there was some fear in the public mind that Madrasis being the most intellectual people would practically secure all the posts in competition... Let them have the posts. They are Indians after all". He felt the ICS "which has done a great deal to develop this country, ought not to be allowed to have members who are poor in commonsense, in ability and in education... the policy of communal representation must stop. It is now creating discontent".

EMPLOYMENT

In the 1940's, as regards the unemployment of educated Indians, Ram Saran Das said, 'I need not dilate much on that subject because everybody knows it and feels the pinch. The majority of our educated young Indians cannot find employment and the Government so far has not been able to find a suitable solution. One of the suitable solutions in my opinion lies in the industrialization of the country".

Again he said, "I have already said that the Board of Scientific and Industrial Research should be put on a permanent basis and yearly allotment should be given to it. In that connection the work which is given to the Institute should be given to Indian nationals in preference over foreigners who start new industries which this Board might recommend'.

MISUSE OF INDIAN RAW PRODUCE

Ram Saran Das wanted to know how the Government was treating India as regards the disposal of raw produce adding the plight of the Indian commercial people is becoming miserable. "The British Government has followed a policy in the case of India's raw produce different from the one they have been following with regard to the primary produce of South Africa, Australia and New Zealand, and even of a non-Empire country like Egypt. With a view to help Egypt's agricultural economy an agreement was entered into with the Egyptian Government under which the British Government contracted to purchase the entire Egyptian crop during the war and one year thereafter at prices considerably higher than of the crop bought during several recent years. What have they done for India?" He added 'prosperity of a country depends upon the economic condition of the masses". He also questioned "why should Indian produce go to foreign countries, be manufactured there and then sent back to India?"

ECONOMIC CONDITIONS

On the Finance Bill, Ram Saran Das claimed that His Majesty's Government was not so generous to India, as it was to other Colonies and Dominions in the matter of purchase of raw produce.

Responding to the question of export of cattle, he said, "...in the Punjab the value of cattle is determined by the weight of its meat... that price has risen to ₹35 a maund. Therefore... it is quite impossible at the price at which cattle are being purchased now in the Punjab, to export any cattle from this province. Punjab... exports cattle to Afghanistan. So, the suggestion that cattle be imported from Afghanistan will never materialise".

"The economic situation in the country is going from

bad to worse.... For some years past I have been advocating in this House the necessity for safeguarding pure ghee from admixture. Various measures were contemplated, but so far no measure has succeeded. It is really difficult to get pure ghee now, and in view of the circumstances which now exist, namely, wholesale slaughter of milch cattle, the position is becoming worse. Even for our religious purposes we cannot get pure ghee.... We find that in the Punjab, in districts where there was no cattle slaughter, such slaughter has been introduced and good milch cattle are also being slaughtered. This is against the assurance which was given in this House by General Hartley on behalf of the Government. But these days I say with regret that the pledges of the Government are sometimes totally violated and actions are taken which are not in the interests of the country as a whole."

He strongly felt "that the Government in England should have charged the cost price for the gold which they are selling through the Reserve Bank of India. It is a pity that Indian silver was sold to the British Isles at a price lower than that which prevailed in India. Why should there be this differential method? Why should silver from India be sold at a lower than that which prevailed in India and why the Reserve Bank sell gold at a price which is almost double that at which it had been purchased from British Government".

INDIAN DOCTORS

With regards to the appointment of foreign refugee doctors being employed in British military hospitals in the 1940's he asked, "Whether it is a fact that some foreign refugee doctors have been employed by the Government as civil practitioners in British Military Hospitals and given pay ranging from ₹600 to ₹1,025, military rank and uniform of R.A.M.C. officers, while Indian doctors employed as civil medical practitioners are given pay ranging from ₹250 to ₹350, without any military rank or uniform? He also questioned if Indian doctors who have joined the I.A.M.C. for service in India only, draw ₹300 to ₹350?"

He questioned whether "British I.M.S. officers drew about ₹13,500 (1,000 pounds) gratuity at the end of 6 years service and about ₹33, 500 (2,500 pounds) at the end of 12 years service; while Indian officers who joined the I.M.S. during the war were given about ₹4,000 at the end of six years and ₹8,000 at the end of 12 years service, i.e 1/3 to ¼ of the amount received by their British colleagues. Also, in regard to the grant of gratuities and other privileges the British officers were taken in permanent service with option to retire at the end of 6 and 12 years service, while Indian officers were taken in temporary or short service".

As a resul,t he said the Indian doctors were not forthcoming for recruitment to the I.A.M.C. as conditions of service were not attractive. With this being so, was the Government prepared to offer attractive terms and conditions of service in the emergency commission Indian doctors who wish to join the arm"'.

HIS LAST SPEECH IN THE COUNCIL OF STATE

In what was perhaps his last speech in the Council of State, after having been the only member with an uninterrupted tenure of nearly 25 years since its conception in Feb 1921, Ram Saran Das took advantage of the Indian Finance Bill 1944 to express his disapproval of the policy of the British Government of undermining India's role in the war effort.

He said, 'I am a cooperator and I wish the war to be won but ....I disapprove of the present policy of the Government. In every country goodwill of the people is essential for the Government of the country. As far as I understand the Government lost Burma because its people lost confidence in the Government and...I must say that in India too, the people are getting restive on seeing that it is becoming the rule of might and not that might was right....orders of the High Courts of Judicature are being ignored and that even the Federal Court has held that the condition under which the country is being at present administered are not satisfactory. The British are well known for their justice and whether that justice is being now administered to or not is a question which I leave the House to decide...Prisoners are released on the order of the judicial authority and as soon as they get out of jail, they are re-arrested under some other Defence of India Regulation. These Defence of India Regulations are the order of the day and anything can be done under these Rules. The voice of the Legislature, of the elected members of the Legislature, is being defied. It would be much better if the Legislatures and the Courts be dissolved and for the time being the country be ruled at the goodwill of those who are in authority....when people are making a sincere War effort and co-operating with the Government there is no justification that the present unjust treatment accorded to them should continue....the British rule... has proved itself to be the best alien rule but in these days the repression of the country under the rule of ordinances and D.F.I. Regulations which is being maintained by them is a question which now is creating resentment in the minds of masses....I am doing whatever is possible to help the Government in war effort and I find that people who do not see eye to eye with me have done many things; so much so that efforts were made to murder one of my responsible officers in order to threaten me to stop co-operation with Government in war effort....I want the war to be won and it is in the interests of India to win the war.... because I do not want the present policy of the Government to continue and the people to be fleeced out as to be made paupers. The taxation should go to the limit of the capacity of the people to pay and to leave them little savings for their existence....I have cleared my position".

The speeches and interventions made by him are an indication that despite his achievements and accomplishments he remained modest, humble and gentle. While thanking the electorate publicly, he vowed to safeguard their interests and was true to his promise. During the last seven years as Leader of the Opposition in the Council of State, he bravely and fearlessly advocated India's cause. This brought him respect and admiration from all quarters and his speeches were regarded as a useful contribution towards India's progress on constitutional lines. He was one of the few eminent Indians trusted and respected by the public. He was strongly opposed to the concept of partition. It is believed that his opposition to the Government as Leader of the Indian Progressive Party Opposition in the Council of State deprived him of a knighthood, on account of difference of views with the British administration.

CHAPTER VIII

DEATH OF R.B. RAM SARAN DAS

Towards the end of his life Ram Saran Das was in poor health. Perhaps his love for sweets, particularly kheer and pinnies, resulted in his being diabetic. In addition he also had high blood pressure. On the domestic front he was under great stress, due perhaps to debts accumulated on account of the lavish lifestyle of various members of his vast family, his own generosity and various commitments. Ultimately, left with no choice he sold off the Nedous Hotel (which had been commercially run) to R. B. Jodha Mal Kuthala for ₹60,00,000. This transaction enabled him to settle his debts. His other numerous properties remained intact. He died on the 23rd November, 1945 at the age of 69, after suffering agonizing pain in his last days. His death made headlines in all the newspapers. The All India Radio kept announcing his death throughout that day. According to his granddaughter Shobha Maini, there was a massive procession for his funeral which was attended by thousands. On that day all the daughters-in-law wore Banarasi saris and grandchildren, new printed satin dresses. A great deal of money and coins were thrown over the 'arthi, which the beggars had a field day collecting from the roadside.

His death and the funeral got wide coverage in the media. After his death his vast property was divided between his five sons. The division of his assets was done in a non-controversial manner. The Arbitrator divided the urban property into five equal parts. Each son was required to pick up a chit of paper in turn. On each chit was written the name of a property and depending on whichever property came to their lot through the chit picked, they became the rightful owners.

The Arbitration Order has been reproduced in an annexure. This was given to me by his grandson, the late Ripudaman, son of his eldest son R.B. Gopal Das. It does not, however, take into account the vast agricultural lands in Punjab particularly in Multan, Lyalpur and Pathankot owned by the family which was separately divided during his lifetime, and neither did it cover their personal assets.

By today's standards it appears unfair that the women did not get any significant share of the assets, though all were educated and given handsome dowries when married. This was in accordance with the laws pertaining to the joint Hindu Family (HUF) of that era. Fighting for the rights of women in India has been an uphill task. More than half a century after his death and independence of the country, the laws have now changed, enabling women to get their rightful share of family inheritance.

With the early death of his younger brother, who had no male heir, Ram Saran Das was the sole inheritor of the family property. He took over the responsibility of his brother's two daughters. He built the vast business empire on the basis of assets inherited from his father R.B. Mela Ram and his own dedication and foresight.

Perhaps he was aptly described thus:

'Ram Saran Das, Member Council of State, 1 Edgerton Road, Lahore, educated in Government College, belongs to a very ancient family whose members were in power for several generations before Maharaja Ranjit Singh's reign in Punjab.

His grandfather, the General of the army during the period of the Bhangi kingdom, had the command of the famous gun, Zamzama. He is a worthy scion of the distinguished family and is one of the leading zamindars and industrialists of the province. He is a member of the Lahore District Board and has subscribed over 8 lacs of rupees in charities." (Unknown)

According to Tahir Kamran, despite his rise and wealth, Ram Saran Das never lost his innate humility and "left an enviable legacy. However, what distinguished Mela Ram and also his son Ram Saran Das was the social plurality which they demonstrated. Electrifying Data Darbar was one big illustration of their non-communal character. Then, at their house (Lal Haveli), all the occasions and festivals were celebrated with equal enthusiasm. Poetry symposiums (Mushairas) were held under their patronage at regular intervals".

With regards to how Ram Saran Das assisted Muslims, Ilyas Chattha writes "In one instance the Hindu businessman R.B. Mela Ram's Ravi Road, Mela Ram Cotton Mill employed half of its workforce from the Muslim Community. Moreover, intercommunity support existed as well. Time to time, the privileged Hindus contributed to Muslim welfare. The business empire of R.B. Mela Ram was in the forefront of such assistance in the city of Lahore. A prime example was the payment for the electrification of Data Ganj Baksh Burban. His son Ram Saran Das provided financial help to a number of Urdu literary journals owned by Muslims".

In short, he wore many hats. He was a contractor, industrialist, land holder, a prominent person in public life, patron of the arts, philanthropist and above all a humanitarian.

MEDIA REPORTS ON DEATH AND FUNERAL PROCESSION OF R.B. RAM SARAN DAS

As the news of his death in the early hours of the morning reached when the newspapers had printed their copies, The Tribune hurriedly changed the first page of its Friday edition of November 23, 1945 to put his photograph along with the following comment.

Lahore Nov. 22. The Hon'ble Rai Bahadur Lala Ram Saran Das, Member of the Council of State, who had been ailing for some time, passed away at 2.5 a.m. on Friday at his residence 1, Egerton Road, Lahore.

The funeral will take place at I p.m. today.

LATE MORNING EDITION

The Tribune

POLICE TWICE OPEN

A. DEMONSTRATORS

KILLED:

RED

Lorries

ire

DEAD

I. N. A.

TR

More E

ALLEGED ILL-TREAT

HORRORS OF ATOMIC WAR

Page 3 of The Tribune Lahore, Saturday 24, 1945 carried the following.

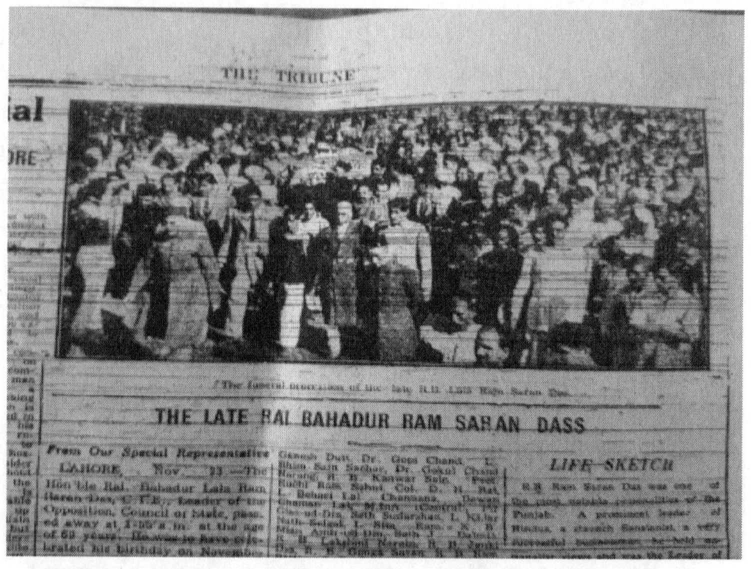

THE TRIBUNE

THE LATE RAI BAHADUR RAM SARAN DASS

From Our Special Representative

LAHORE, Nov. 23.—The Hon'ble Rai Bahadur Lala Ram Saran Das, C.I.E., Leader of the Opposition, Council of State, passed away at 1.55 a.m. at the age of 69 years. He was to have celebrated his birthday on Novem-

LIFE SKETCH

R.B. Ram Saran Das was one of ... Punjab. A prominent leader of Hindus, a staunch Sanatanist, a very successful businessman ...

The Late Rai Bahadur Ram Saran Das

From Our Special Correspondent

Lahore Nov. 23. The Hon'ble Rai Bahadur Lala Ram Saran Das, C.I.E. Leader of the Opposition, Council of State, passed away at 1.55 a.m. at the age of 69 years. He was to have celebrated his birthday on November 25. The end that came suddenly followed a sudden deterioration in his condition which took a bad turn the day before yesterday. He had not been keeping well for a pretty long time, but since the beginning of this month he had recovered and showed definite improvement in his health. In fact he thought that he had now fully recovered so much that he had begun to take a keen interest in the election of his son, Rai Bahadur Gopal Das, for the Provincial Assembly.

But about a week back, the condition of his health again took a bad turn and ever since November 14 his condition had been serious. He had suffered from heart trouble for about two years, but he had been able to resist his ailment successfully.

The end was peaceful and at the time were present by his bedside Rani Sahiba (his wife), his eldest son R.B. Gopal Das and one of his three daughters. Soon after he died his other sons, Flight Lt. Rup Chand, Mr. Ravi Shanker. Mr. Jagdish Chander, Mr. Rajeshwar and his second daughter came in to see their father dead.

Till midnight R.B. Gopal Das had been sitting by the side of his father when he went into the adjoining room for a short time only and his sister was sitting by her father's bed side. At about 12.30 a.m. R.B. Gopal Das was called in. He rushed into the room of his father and found him vomiting blood. He then began to sink. Within the next twenty minutes, his condition became grave and at five minutes to two he passed away peacefully.

With the death of R.B. Ram Saran Das a distinguished member of that old order, which unhappily is fading away, which has been held in the highest esteem by people of all communities irrespective of their political creeds or religious faiths has passed away. By his death yet another eminent Punjabee has crossed over into the unknown realm where some other eminent Punjabees went away during this year. The Punjab is getting poorer every day of men who could wield influence on public life and the province is even more poor today.

'Rai Ram Saran Das' , this was how the people of Lahore remembered Hon'ble Rai Bahadur Ram Saran Das and they used to talk of his 'unfathomed' riches and the charities he gave for religious purposes. Though an orthodox by religious faith, he did not allow himself to be carried away by any communal consideration in the matter of help to the needy.

The Premier Lt. Col. Khizar Hyat Khan, Mian Abdul Haye, Mr. Justice Din Mohammed. Mr. Justice Mehr Chand Mahajan. Mr. Justice Ram Lal, Mr. Justice Teja Singh and Mr. H.D. Dhanot, Chief Secretary were among the large number of people who called at the residence of the late R.B. Ram Saran Das and offered their condolences to R.B. Gopal Das and his other sons.

A very large number of prominent citizens representing various organisations and institutions as also leaders of all the communities also visited 1, Egerton Road to offer their condolences to the bereaved family. All Sanatanist Institutions, the S.D. College, the S.D. Schools, the office of the S.D. Pratinidhi Sabha and all allied organisations were closed as a mark of respect to the memory of the late R.B. Ram Saean Das.

Funeral Procession

The body of R.B. Ram Saran Das, Leader of Opposition, Council of State, was cremated this evening when the funeral procession terminated at the 'Shamshan Bhumi' after covering a distance of about five miles from the late Rai Bahadur's residence at 1, Egerton Road. The cremation ceremony was performed according to the strict Sanatanist rites in the presence of a huge gathering of citizens of Lahore, who included besides a large number of ladies, people representing various communities and political creeds. Among those who followed the procession and attended the funeral were Sir Manohar Lal, Finance Minister Punjab Ch. Tika Ram, Revenue Minister Punjab, Mr. Justice Mehr Chand Mahajan, Mr. Justice Ram Lal, S.B. Mohan Singh, Goswami Ganesh Dutt, Dr. Gopi Chand, L Bhim Sain Sachar, Dr. Gokul Chand Narang, R.B.

Kanwar Sain, Prof. Ruchi Ram Sahni, Col D.H. Rai. L Behari Lal Channana, Dewan Chaman Lal, M.L.A. (Central) Pir Gias-ud-Din, Seth Sudarshan, L Kidar Nath Saigol. L Sita Ram, K.B. Mian Amir-ud-Din, Seth J. Dalmia, R.B. Lakshmi Narain, R.B. Janki Das, R.B. Ganga Saran, R.B. Ram Rattan, S.B. Prabh Singh Chawla, Mr. Yodh Raj, Mr. M.R. Kohli. Dr. Nihal Chand, R.B. Dr. Ganesh Das Kapur, R.B. Dr. Mathra Das, R.B. Dr. Maharaj Krishan, Dr. Bhagat Ram Khanna, Dr. Jamait Singh, Dr. Randhir Singh, Principal D.N. Bhalla, Principal P.M. Maulik, Malik J.L. Kapur, Mr. D. R. Sawhney, Kh. Dil Mohd, K.B. Mohd Naqf, Prof. Ganga Ram Kohli, Prof. M.C. Sethi, Seth Lachman Das, Sardar Devinder Singh Additional District Magistrate Mr. Tek Chand, R.S. Narsingh Das, Lala Hari Chand Puri and members of the S.D. College staff and school staff.

The procession which started from the Egerton Road exactly at 1 p.m. wended its way through the Mall after passing from in front of the Assembly buildings.

The funeral procession entered the Anarkali and went into the city through the Lahori Gate and after passing through the main bazaars emerged out of the city from the Water Works Chowk side and terminated at the cremation grounds after a period of three hours.

The bazaars in the city on the route of the procession were all closed and the Muslim shopkeepers in the Lahori Gate, Chauk Matti, also kept their shops closed as a mark of respect to the memory of the Late R.B. Ram Saran Das. All along the route from the Egerton Road right upto the cremation grounds flowers were showered on the 'arthi' and rose water was sprinkled in plenty by the people who lined the route or stood in front of the closed shops in the city. In the city bandwalas played the mourning tunes as the procession passed in front of their quarters.

At the Charring Cross Lala Behari Lal Channana, L Ram Prakash and L Panna Lal placed wreaths on behalf of the Punjab Beepar Mandal. L Bhim Sain Sacchar offered floral tribute to the departed Chairman of the Sunlight Insurance Company as the procession stood in front of the Sunlight Buildings.

The R.B. Ram Saran Das was a Director of the Central Bank and garlands were placed on the 'arthi' by Mr. Jariwala on behalf of the bank.

Similarly, flowers were placed on the 'arthi' by Mr. Dhawan on behalf of the city branch of the Central Bank.

As the procession emerged out of the city Goswamu Ganesh Dutt placed wreaths on the 'arthi' on behalf of the Sanatan Dharam Pratinidhi Sabha and its allied organisation.

At the cremation grounds fire was set to the pier by R.B. Gopal Das eldest son of the late R.B. Ram Saran Das and within the next few moments it was all over.

As a mark of respect to the memory of the late Rai Bahadur the following business concerns, with which he was connected were closed and the members of their staff passed condolence resolutions. The Sunlight of India Insurance Co., The Bharat Fire and General Insurance Co and the Investors Trust Ltd.

Deep sympathies are being expressed with R.B. Gopal Das Flight Lt. Rup Chand and their 3 brothers and a large number of telegrams have been received from out stations

PROF. ABDUL MAJID KHAN'S TRIBUTE

The late R.B. Ram Saran Das was a prince among the philanthropists of Punjab. A great friend of the late Sir Muhammad Shafi and Fazl Husain, he firmly believed in the saying that difference of opinion that springs from intellectual integrity or honesty of purpose is a blessing in disguise and is something to be welcomed. Absolutely immune from the irritating effects of the intoxication of wealth, altogether unassuming, in many ways he possessed a pleasant personality and was widely respected for the sweetness of his temperament and suavity of his manners.

S.D. EDUCATIONAL INSTITUTIONS TO CLOSE ON NOV 24

Lahore Nov. 23. Goswami Ganesh Dutt writes: As a mark of respect to the memory of Late R.B. Ram Saran Das all Sanatan Dharam Sabhas and educational institutions should close institutions on Nov. 24. Public meetings should be held to mourn the irreparable loss and condolence resolutions should be passed. Mass prayers should also be arranged for the departed soul.

LIFE SKETCH

R.B. Ram Saran Das was one of the most notable personalities of Punjab. A prominent leader of Hindus, a staunch Sanatanist, a very successful businessman, he held nationalist views and was the Leader of the Opposition in the Council of State.

Born in Lahore on November 26, 1876, L (Lala) Ram Saran Das belonged to a leading ancient family, the members of which were in power for several generations before Maharaj Ranjit Singh;s reign in Punjab. His great-grand-father once commanded the well known cannon "Zamzama". His father R.B. Mela Ram was a pioneer businessman of the Punjab and a great philanthropist, enjoying enviable social distinction at the hands of all including Indian princes.

While still a lad of 14, L Ram Saran Das's father died leaving him to take charge of the huge estates vast contracts and lands. The young Ram Saran Das studied in Central Model School and then in the Government College, Lahore, but though good at books, he was forced to leave college without taking a degree in view of the heavy responsibilities which he was suddenly called upon to shoulder. The hard working, far sighted person that he was he soon became a leading figure in commercial circles and by dint of his labour amassed a fortune. He started the first spinning and weaving mill in the Punjab in 1897, known as Mela Ram Cotton Mills, employing over 1,000 hands.

LEADING INDUSTRIALIST

The Rai Bahadur was associated with a large number of commercial firms and was regarded as a foremost industrialist. He was Director of the Imperial Bank of India, Chairman of the Advisory Committee Central Bank of India (Punjab Branches) was a member U.P. Industrial Banking Enquiry Committee and delegate of the session of Associated Chambers of British Empire Federation which met in London in 1933. He was General President of the Sanatan Dharma College, Managing Committee and President of the S.D.Pratanidhi Sabha.

L Ram Saran Das was elected to the old Punjab Legislative Council in 1918 and did very creditable work. He had been a member of the Council of State since 1920 and safeguarded the interests of the Hindus of the Punjab. His speeches in the Legislature were well supported with facts and figures and were carefully listened to by all sections of the House. He had been the Leader of the Opposition in the Council of State for the last 7 years.

RESPECTED BY ALL COMMUNITIES

L Ram Saran Das as Joint Secretary of the Kangra Valley Earthquake Relief Committee rendered very valuable service to the unfortunate victim of the 1905 earthquake.

The Rai Bahadur was a person with a great religious bent of mind and devoted several hours everyday to the performance of religious duties and prayers. He had studied the sacred books of the Hindus thoroughly and also read the holy books of Muslims, the Sikhs and of other religions. He respected all beliefs and had no prejudices against any religion. He was respected by members of all communities.

The late Rai Bahadur was a great admirer of Indian music and listened to masters of classical music with rapt attention. He was himself conversant with the technique of Indian music.

Very alert, accurate and active in his business and public life, he was nevertheless of sober and thoughtful temperament. He was very fond of travelling and had visited several foreign countries, including Britain, the European continent, Egypt, Dutch East Indies, Java, Bali Malaya, Siam, Indo-China, Burma and Ceylon. Throughout his wide travels in the East and the West he retained the typical Indian dress.

R.B. Ram Saran Das had a charitable disposition and was a great philanthropist. Hundreds of persons in Lahore and other places have benefitted from his charities and will remember him with gratitude. His charities ran into a million rupees and included handsome grants to educational institutions, hospitals and various public bodies.

(The Tribune, November 24, 1945)

Condolence Meetings

During the next few days following his death, newspapers carried tributes, resolutions and other articles.

CHAPTER IX

PARTITION 1947

The majority community at the time of partition in Lahore were the Muslims. At the onset of the 20th century, the prosperous Hindus and Sikhs owned most of the property in the city. Taking advantage of modern education and adapting to the changing times, both these communities had a headstart over the Muslims. This farsightedness helped them to be better placed within the developing capitalist economy. The Muslims lagged behind, on account of a conservative outlook, but with the government policy of job reservation their fortunes underwent a change.

The acute economic discrepancy between the Muslims and non-Muslims was one of the primary causes of discontent. The Muslims, felt vulnerable in a Hindu dominated society and their insecurity and apprehensiveness bubbled to the surface with the call for a separate state.

Initially religious slogans were given belligerent overtones. The Muslim, 'Naara-e-Takbeer, Allah-o- Akbar', the Hindu 'Har har Mahadev" and the Sikhs "Jo bole so nihal. Sat sri akal" filled the air. Stones would be hurled, resulting in many being injured. This display of religious intolerance created a sense of insecurity amongst all communities. More aggressive and organised attacks followed and several innocent bystanders were stabbed to death. The police, in order to maintain some semblance of law and order, would fire to disperse crowds.

With the British taking no strong measures to control the situation, the communities became further emboldened. Soon Muslims started attacking Hindus in areas where the Hindus were in a minority and likewise Hindus attacked Muslims in areas where they were in majority. The result was sad as friends and neighbours became foes overnight. Communal violence and tension rose in the winter of 1945-46 and the March of 1947 witnessed the first serious communal clashes.

The last British Viceroy, Mountbatten, arrived in India on March 22, 1947. Charged with overseeing the transfer of power and viewing the prevalent volatile situation, he pre-empted the partition to 14-15 August, 1947. In June Cyril Radcliffe, a talented Barrister, was asked to chair two Boundary Commissions-Bengal and Punjab. Unfortunately Radcliffe had no knowledge of India and had little time to be apprised of the complex situation.

Awards of the Boundary Commission were ready by 12/13 August. However, at the Viceroys 69th Staff Meeting on 9th August, a decision was taken not to declare the Awards before Independence Day. The British feared that an earlier publication would mean the British would have to bear the responsibility of the violence that would follow, reducing goodwill towards them.

The British had internally sent telegrams regarding the Awards on 14 August, that meetings with the Indian leaders would take place on the 16th with public announcements made on August 17th.

The decision significantly meant that on Independence Day, people along the border had no idea which country they belonged to.

As Mountbatten was required to be present at both ceremonies as the Representative of the British Crown, a compromise was made. Pakistan declared independence on 14 August and India a day later on the 15th.

The climax was reached at midnight with Nehru's famous speech. The Hindustan Times of August 15 reported slogans like Mahatma Gandhi ki Jai filled the air. The birth of the nation, India, was witnessed by representatives from the USA, Canada, China, Australia and other countries.

The 'Dawn' likewise reported happenings across the boundary in Pakistan.

The flood gates thereafter opened from mid August to November.

With no organised steps taken by the government to maintain law and order following the announcement, the situation ran out of control. Violence became widespread, affecting all segments of society targeting helpless victims. Children watched parents being burnt to death and many were kidnapped. Women were abducted, humiliated, raped and tortured. Several chose to jump into wells to save their honour. Men were murdered mercilessly. Groups of men belonging to different communities carried blazing sticks and set fire to whatever came in their way. Properties were looted, burnt and destroyed. Some villages were completely exterminated. Families in desperation sought sanctuaries wherever they could. Sadly the situation worsened with the riots spinning out of control and people were left to fend for their survival as the government appeared to be paralysed.

According to Lt. Gen. Barney White-Spanner the people were divided along communal and linguistic lines and the strong emotions and rage expressed were unimaginable. Neighbours killed each other while friends turned a blind eye. Sadly the police and the administration neglected their call of duty. This according to him was one of the worst cases of suffering in human history with systematic mutilation and murder on both sides.

Thousands fled in terror, abandoning their homes and belongings. Rendered homeless, they were forced to leave carrying with them only memories. There was no time to mourn the death of a dear one. Nor was it easy to find a family member one was separated from. A feeling of total helplessness overtook all, as the need of the hour was simply to survive.

This huge demographic upheaval created the single biggest refugee movement in history. Trains were packed with passengers clueless of their final destination. There were horrifying tales of ghost trains arriving full of dead bodies as thousands were butchered enroute. An overwhelming smell of rotting corpses filled the air. Endless lines of bullock carts, laden with people made their way through searing heat and torrential rains. Thousands crossed the border in deplorable conditions. Some suffered acute physical stress, due to unavailability of any form of transport and dependent on their own two feet. Along the way many lost their few belongings which were either stolen or confiscated. There was no shelter, no food, no sanitation or water. Exhaustion, starvation, disease and death haunted them at every step.

The transition led to displacement and sadly alienation, with people who through generations had been neighbours and friends.

The outcome was a mass exodus of humanity. Some decided to stay against all odds, perhaps due to economic reasons, pragmatism or the belief that things would soon return to normal. It is indeed sad that countless lives were lost due to the decision of a few politicians. The British who had ruled with an iron hand could have made this transition orderly and prevented the biggest bloodbath in history. Their policy of divide and rule made them confident that they would have the upper hand by eventually playing mediator between two disputing nations.

By the end, 12 million refugees had crossed in both directions of the newly created Radcliffe Line, which served as the line of demarcation dividing the countries, India and Pakistan. As Radcliffe had arrived in India only a short while before, with no knowledge of the sub-continent as he had never been to India. However, there had been hope that his decision would be non-biased. It was said that on witnessing the violent bloodshed as a result of his verdict, he was shaken, refused to accept the salary due to him and returned to England immediately. Large number of Muslims chose to remain in India rather than migrate to Pakistan. Hindus and Sikhs from Punjab and the North-West Frontier Province had to leave for India, while some Hindus stayed behind in interior Sindh and East Pakistan. Estimates of the casualties varied. A figure of half a million was mentioned, but it is believed that the correct figure could have been more likely 200,000.

Rumours of vicious massacres were far from reassuring and people sought shelter in fast growing refugee camps. None had anticipated the scale of tragedy wrought by the partition. Many still believed that this was a temporary situation and they would return to their homeland once matters were settled.

But the reality of partition could not be undone and with the passage of time it soon became evident that the state of affairs was permanent. India had been divided into two sovereign states—India and Pakistan. With each passing day, any hope they had of returning to their homes became dimmer and gradually faded away. They had no choice but to accept the finality of partition. There was a general feeling of despair at the thought of starting life afresh in an alien city. To adjust to a completely new environment could not have been easy.

In the new India post 1947, a Department of Resettlement was set up in Jullunder, whose principal task was to tackle the problem of rehabilitation. However, the relief efforts proved inadequate. With the onslaught of a continuing stream of refugees, tents were set up and makeshift kitchens struggled to provide meals. Providing elementary first aid to the injured was proving difficult and taking care of those in critical condition was an impossible task. The deplorable sanitary conditions led to the outbreak of cholera, adding to the plight of the refugees.

The partition took many unaware. Many families on a summer vacation in the hill-side resorts of the Himalayas were unaware of the turbulence being unleashed. At the time of partition, my grandmother and family were vacationing in the summer capital of British India, Simla. The abrupt decision to partition the country and be told you could never return to your home, your possessions lost forever must have come as a huge shock and a devastating blow. Unexpectedly being ejected from your birthplace, where you had expected to spend the rest of your life and an uncertain future facing you must have made one agonizingly helpless.

However, to the credit of the refugees, those profoundly difficult times were faced stoically. There are few examples in history when penniless refugees, arriving on a large scale, immediately set about rehabilitating themselves. Initially refugee camps located in different places such as Nilokheri, Faridabad and on the outskirts of Delhi served as home, resulting in the population of Delhi doubling overnight. Some found refuge in the homes of family and friends. But this was a short lived, as they soon realised they were a burden. The concept of a pragmatic approach to adapt to the present circumstances, and start a new life took precedence. Initially, the influx of refugees was resented by the locals, who feared competition for a livelihood. The refugees, in order to survive had no choice but to take any job at whatever pay. Some restarted work based on their own skills and old professions, while others grabbed new opportunities. Some sold the little gold they had carried for ₹20 for a tola. Sheer hard work and determination moulded them into the people they are today. Despite all difficulties it was these very people who were eventually able to rehabilitate themselves in their new environment.

Following the partition everything had to be divided between the two countries. This proved to be a tedious and contentious process. Railways that had formed the backbone of the British Empire were divided. This pertained to the extensive network of tracks, locomotives, coaches and personnel. The armed forces too were split. Communities lost access to religious sites—the Muslims to Ajmer Sharif and Nizamuddin, Hindus to the Katas Raj Temple near Rawalpindi, Sikhs to Nankana Sahib, Panja Sahib and Patti Sahib and Buddhists to Stupas and Monastries in Taxila, Takh-e-Bahi. The Jains transported their idols by air from Multan. These are displayed in Sri Digambar Jain Lal Mandir in Delhi. Relics of Mohenjodaro too were divided and on the cultural front both countries lost out on their favourite artists due to the division.

Meanwhile, the Government set about making new townships and establishing vocational training centres for the unemployed. A system to re-compensate property, was begun. Food rations too were defined.

Within a short span of a few years new shops, factories and workplaces came up, which later matched with the best in the country. At that time, individual prestige took a back seat against the spirit and determination to resettle. A new tapestry, woven and embroidered, enabled the new India to establish itself as a vibrant country. Despite their initial inhibitions, credit must also be given to the local residents who eventually helped and encouraged the refugees in their endeavours. The word refugee soon disappeared from their title in India. In Pakistan, however, the Muslims who went from India are still after seven decades referred to as Mohajirs or refugees.

My parents, prior to partition, had travelled to Europe and America, crossing the Atlantic by ship—the Queen Mary and Queen Elizabeth respectively. Hearing of the unexpected events back home, they hastily returned from Europe. Flights in those days were of a short duration as they required refuelling, leaving my parents no option but to halt in an atmosphere of intense fear and hostility in Karachi. Pleading with the authorities at the airport to ensure safe travel to Delhi, they offered whatever was in their possession, their money, shopping and jewellery. The authorities concerned, assured them that not only would they leave safely, but together with all their belongings. However, they were cautioned while staying in a Karachi hotel, not to contact any friend for their own safety. With the situation out of hand and emotions running high, no one knew who was a friend or a foe. Most of the waiters of the hotel recognized my father, as in the past he had often stayed in that hotel, making the situation all the more tense. But, despite the vicious and brutal turn events had taken, there were good Samaritans too. My parents caught the flight the following day with their baggage to Delhi and were reunited with the family.

The irony of history was that Mahatma Gandhi the Father of the Indian Nation was assassinated on January 30, 1948, five months after partition, and Jinnah the Father of the Pakistan Nation died (due to an illness which was a closely guarded secret) on September 11, 1948, eight months after Gandhi. Both died the year following partition.

After partition, our family also migrated to Delhi where life had to now start afresh. The elder two sons, already in their forties, had the advantage of being settled in their professions prior to partition. R.B. Gopal Das, who had followed in the footsteps of his father, be it in business or public life was a member of the Punjab Legislative Assembly in Lahore. His son Inderjit related that his father, Gopal Das, was amongst those who had received Prince Edward VIII in 1921-22 during his visit to India. In the changed circumstances, Gopal Das, with his wide experience, continued his public life but preferred to stay in the cooler climes of the hill stations in properties he had inherited from his father.

Decades later when we were on our first posting in Islamabad in the late 1970's, I had hosted a lunch for Mrs. Sathe, wife of the visiting Indian Foreign Secretary. At lunch the wife of the then Secretary General of the Pakistan Foreign Office, Shahnawaz, enquired if we could help put her in touch with a family they had been close to. She said her father had been presented with a beautiful writing desk from this dear friend, which she now had in her possession. On hearing the name R. B. Gopal Das son of R. B. Ram Saran Das, I told her that the former was my father's elder brother and the latter my grandfather. Thereafter she and her husband were always exceedingly warm towards us.

The second son, Wing Cmdr. Rup Chand had a passion for flying. According to Khizr Tiwana his close friend, Rup

Chand possessed one of the first private planes. Rup Chand also founded the Flying Club of Lahore. After the partition, he was appointed India's first Ambassador to Afghanistan in 1947 by Pandit Jawahar Lal Nehru as a political appointee.

On our second posting to Pakistan, in the early 1990's, we met in Islamabad a cousin of the King of Afghanistan who was residing in France. He was visiting with the renewed hope of returning to Afghanistan with the King who had till now been living in exile in Rome. Recalling the old days in Kabul, he described a parallel darbar to the King's held by India's first Ambassador, Wing Cmdr Rup Chand, to Afghanistan and was full of praise of the generous hospitality received.

Both R.B. Gopal Das and Rup Chand inherited substantial property and agricultural lands in what became India.

The compensation my grandmother received from the government in lieu of property lost due to partition was 2 lakhs. All the five sons also got 2 lakhs each. In addition my father and his two brothers got farm lands in Hissar. Later my father, Jagdish Chander, and his elder brother Ravi Shanker bought farm lands in the Terai region of Rampur.

For the younger three, who were at that time in their twenties, life had to start afresh. Each son rehabilitated himself on coming to Delhi. The eldest, Ravi Shanker, took to farming in the newly acquired lands in the Terai region. My father, Jagdish Chander joined the South India Insurance which subsequently became the New India Insurance. The youngest, Rajeshwar Bali, a keen tennis player took to photography and set up a company known as 'Midas.'

Chapter X

MY PATERNAL GRANDMOTHER AND AFTERMATH OF PARTITION

My grandfather died before I was born, but I have vivid memories of my grandmother. As my grandfather had married a second time after the death of his first wife, my grandmother was much younger than him. According to my uncle Rajeshwar, he fondly called her 'Chaudhry Sahib'. A noble, gentle and soft spoken lady, she was liked by all.

My uncle, Rajeshwar, with his passion for photography, often showed us films taken at functions in their house in Edgerton Road, pre-partition Lahore. This was always a treat. A great deal of excitement was generated amongst us grand children when the screen together with the projector was set up in the garden of our Prithvi-raj Road house in Delhi. It was fun seeing our parents and other members of the family when they were younger. Recognizing anyone familiar lead to enthusiastic shouts followed by gleeful laughter. We were always amazed to see our grandmother whom we affectionately called 'Phaboji' on the screen wearing richly coloured saris and jewellery. It seemed as though she belonged to a different era—a total contrast to her present appearance. Having renounced everything after the death of her husband, she had entered a new phase of life, dressed only in a white or saffron sari, without a trace of jewellery.

My grandmother and her three sons, rented a house on a long term lease on Prithvi-raj Road, but never thought of buying the property as they thought they might return to Lahore. I was told that my grandmother initially could not reconcile to the new environment, but with the passage of time she accepted the changed circumstances.

After having suffered two simultaneous losses, the death of her husband and the consequences of partition, she became deeply religious, finding solace in the name of God. Her day started at dawn with prayers and later a visit to the temple. She contributed generously to the building of a large temple on the banks of the river Jumna in old Delhi. She also had a section made for the Brahmcharis of the temple. Never wanting any acknowledgement for the donation, she refused to have a plaque carrying her name on display. However, after her death, the then head priest of the temple approached her three sons, saying they wanted to recognize her contribution publicly, and sought permission to put up a plaque. All three declined, saying that if their mother had not wanted it, her wishes should be respected. However, the head priest had her name written in the Brahmchari section as the donor.

As her eldest grand-daughter, I often accompanied her to the temple on holidays. After the prayers in a large hall a little time was spent with the holy men of the temple. Each sat in a separate small room where they held discourses. These were constantly full of people. Several questions were raised with learned answers given in response.

Annually Ram Naomi would be celebrated in the temple with great fanfare. My grand-mother always hosted the lunch in the temple on this day. We as a family would wait till the priests, the brahmcharis and others had eaten. The family would sit on the jute matting that covered the floor. Much to

Mohan Kaur (middle) with Indira Gandhi and Bimla Thapar (daughter of Rup Kaur), wife of Gen. P.N. Thapar, Chief of Army Staff

our delight food would be served on banana leaves and water in earthernware cups. For us this was a novelty. The vegetarian food carried and served by volunteers in large buckets, was always delicious.

My grandmother had become a total vegetarian. Though no other member of the family was a vegetarian, we ate our meals together in silver thalis. I recall several extended members of the family visiting my grandmother. She would always receive them warmly and was genuinely happy to see them. I too would spend time with them and as such became close to them. Kind and caring she was sensitive to the feelings of others.

I joined Loretto Convent Tara Hall, a school in Simla, as a boarder at the age of four. My mother had been an ex-student

Rup Kaur with husband Bashi Ram Sehgal

of the school and I had accompanied her when she took a diplomat's daughter for admission. Happy at the affectionate attention the Irish nuns paid me as the daughter of an ex-student, I apparently insisted on joining the school. My mother gave in to my whim and stayed for two months at the Oberoi Cecil Hotel, ready to take me back to Delhi once she thought I had had my fill. I, however, chose to stay on and did so for the next four years. It was at my grandmother's insistence that I was withdrawn. She was concerned that with spending nine months of the year in the boarding school, my mother tongue was endangered as my communication in Hindi became more limited with each passing year. Thereafter I continued my studies in the Convent of Jesus and Mary in Delhi.

On return to Delhi, I spent prime time with my grandmother. She would relate mythological stories of the Mahabharata and Gita. I often accompanied her when she went to her elder son Ravi Shanker in Nainital, where he had rented a house, due

Wife of R.B. Ram Saran Das. Author's grandmother

to its close proximity to the Terai farmlands.

I do not recall ever seeing my grandmother angry. She was gentle, warm, soft spoken and amazingly patient. She never scolded us but corrected us gently by explaining the pros and cons of any action. Every birthday she presented me with a jewellery piece which I wore for a brief spell during the party. At that time I never appreciated her gift and would sulkily tell her that other grandmothers' gave ₹21 or progressively ₹31 for the birthdays of their grandchildren. Amused she would hand that amount over to me, with which I would happily buy Enid Blyton books followed by more mature books with the passing years. It was more than a decade after her death that

I appreciated the gifts given me over the years. Her locker was opened twelve years after her death. Lakshmanji of Kanjimull jewellers evaluated her jewels before dividing them into three parts.

Amazingly, no member of my family talked about Lahore in terms of the status of the family. My grandmother never spoke about the past and neither did my father or his brothers. My mother had been married just a short while before partition, so her experience within the family was limited. We grew up in Delhi, where the family started life afresh and were totally unaware of the family's standing in the city they had left behind. Perhaps not talking about the past was all for the best. It made our growing years normal, rather than having illusions or yearning for a life that had evaded us. Our outlook was grounded having been brought up on values of the present. Even collectively in the joint family there was no reference to the past. Perhaps this was also because several years had already lapsed since partition. However, despite whatever we may have lost as a result of partition, I recall our childhood in Delhi as being a happy and carefree one.

The years gradually took their toll on my grandmother. In 1961, while on a summer vacation to Simla, she started running low grade fever. On return to Delhi she was diagnosed as having cancer. Within a short period of time her condition deteriorated and she started losing weight and became very weak. I will never forget how two days before her death the head priest from the temple came to visit and said two days later would be a good time for her to go. I was quite aghast when I heard him say so. But she did die, unbelievably, two days later. We were all shattered and that was the only time I saw my father cry.

Her death was the end of an era for the family.

ANNEXURE 1

EXTRACTED ARTICLE ON R. B. RAM SARAN DAS WRITTEN BY P.D. SAGGI FROM THE BOOK PUNJAB'S EMINENT HINDUS EDITED BY N. B. SEN AND PUBLISHED BY NEW BOOK SOCIETY, LAHORE (DECEMBER 1943)

R.B.L. RAM SARAN DAS
(By Mr. P. D. Saggi, B.A. (Hons.) Lahore

Unassuming in manners, simple in dress and gentle in his talk, the Hon'ble Rai Bahadur Lala Ram Saran Das, C.I.E., Leader of the Opposition in the Council of State, is one of the most notable personalities of this province. He is liked by persons of all communities, for he is sincere, hospitable and full of human sympathy for his fellow beings.

Born in Lahore on the 26th November, 1876, L Ram Saran Das belongs to a family which attained great distinction in the days before the Punjab came under the rule of Maharaja Ranjit Singh. His great grand-father, Diwan Das Mal, who flourished from 1747-1798 was a Commander of the Artillery under the Bhattis. The Zamzama, a historical cannon on the Lower Mall, was then under his command. His personal qualities of mind and body helped him to achieve various distinctions which brought him great respect in the State. The Diwan led a very heroic life. He had one son, Diwan Dhanpat Rai, born in 1796.

Two years later, Diwan Das Mal died. Shortly after his death, Maharaja Ranjit Singh marched on Lahore and attained the sovereignty of the Punjab. In the changes that followed, all the jagirs and properties of the late Diwan were confiscated and the surviving members of his family were ordered to be massacred. His maternal grandfather secretly carried away the baby-Dhanpat Rai- from Lahore to Batala, where he nourished him in obscurity at great personal risk. Diwan Dhanpat Rai had to lead his entire life in comparative poverty, but he was a contented fellow and had full faith in the dictates of Nature. He married in a respectable Khattriya family and had two sons-Lala Ram Dyal, born in 1817 and Lala Mela Ram, born in 1832. The return of the fortunes and prestige of the family was mainly due to his younger son, Mela Ram, during whose life-time the Punjab passed from the domain of the Khalsa to that of the British. Lala Mela Ram had the adaptability and courage to take advantage of the changed circumstances which he turned to his favour.

He started life as a contractor and by dint of his honesty, integrity and hard work rose to the top of his profession. The zeal and energy which he possessed in an abundant measure, coupled with his earnest desire to revive the old glories of his once magnificent family, endeared him to his officers, colleagues and subordinates. He took the entire contract of the Amritsar-Pathankote Railway, including iron-work, sleepers and masonry, which he finished with his characteristic energy well within the contracted time. The Government was much pleased at his resourcefulness and granted him a special reward of ₹50,000—for this performance. In February 1869, he attained the distinction of being appointed a 'Darbari', and seventeen years later, was honoured with the title of "Rai Bahadur". Even though his income was enormous, his charities were no less; roughly estimated, these amounted to a million of rupees. He built a magnificent tank near the Lahore

Railway Station and sunk many wells in different towns of this province. There wasa ahostel to feed the poor and a shop to distribute free flour to beggars ,were started by him in Lahore. His donations to public institutions under Government control were ₹24,000/- to Delhi Hospital (1864), ₹15,000/- to Central Training College, Lahore (1886) and ₹15,000/_ to the Lady Dufferin Hospital for Women (1886). Rai Bahadur Lala Mela Ram enjoyed great social distinctions at the hands of all, and even the Rajas and Maharajas of various Indian States showed him great courtesy and attention at their Durbars. He died on the 10th of April 1890, leaving behind him two minor sons, the elder being Lala Ram Saran Das.

Thus at the age of 14, the young boy was deprived of the blessings of his father. At that time he was studying in the Central Model School. After matriculating in 1897, he joined the Government College, Lahore where he took Science, Sanskrit and History. In 1896, when his uncle died he had to discontinue studies without taking a degree. His tutors were unwilling to part with him, for he was a sober and thoughtful boy with inclinations towards deep study of various subjects. But there was no alternative. He was then the only male member of the family and it was necessary for him to devote all his attention towards the management of his father's vast estates, contracts and zamindari. Therefore, at a very young age, Lala Ram Saran Das had to shoulder heavy responsibilities. But he gave a good account of himself by devoting his entire time, attention and energies towards the self-imposed task and the results were marvellous. Very soon he acquired a deep insight into business affairs and with the help of his vast resources coupled with his own skill and industry, he started the first Spinning and Weaving mill in this province. This mill was formally opened in 1897 by Sir Dennis

Fitzpatric, the then Lieutenant Governor of the Punjab, and is today employing more than one thousand hands. It would be interesting to mention here that at one time, Rai Bahadur Ram Saran Das himself worked in this mill as a Dispatcher, Correspondence-Clerk and Accountant. Besides, he gained practical experience as a Mechanical and Civil Engineer and is now considered to be a good Engineer. Not only that. He did everything to extend his business in various ways. Once he undertook large contracts for the construction of a Division of the Nagda-Mathura Railway where he was employing about 12,000 men at a time.

Various bridges, railway lines and magnificent buildings have been constructed by his firm, known as Messrs. R.B. Mela Ram & Sons, Lahore.

Along with his vast business activities and commercial enterprises, he has always been taking a keen and active interest in public life. At the age of 22, he was nominated a member of the District Board, Lahore and held that office creditably for 20 years. He also worked as a Municipal Commissioner for about 18 years. In 1909, the title of "Rai Sahib" was conferred on him and the next year he became Rai Bahadur. In 1914, he was awarded the Kaiser-i-Hind Gold Medal and in 1916 was honoured with the "C.I.E.". Two years later, under the Montford Reforms, he was elected to the Punjab Legislative Council, as it was then called, and did valuable work there. He used to make fine speeches, supported by facts and figures, in every session and his views were received with due attention by all concerned.

It was in 1920 that the Rai Bahadur came into limelight by his election to the Council of State. Only one seat is allotted to the Hindus of this province and there were seven more candidates in the field, including the late Harkishen Lal. It was really a fight between two giants and Lala Ram Saran Das surprised his friends and foes alike by polling single handed more votes than all the votes of his seven rivals put together. This was a great victory in the history of elections in this province. But it made the Rai Bahadur all the more humble and gentle and after thanking the electorate publicly he promised to safeguard their interests and there is no doubt that he has been true to his professions. His brave and fearless advocacy of India's cause, during the last six years, as Leader of the Opposition in the Council of State, has brought him respect and admiration from all quarters. His speeches have generally been regarded as a useful contribution towards India's progress on constitutional lines.

Several years ago, the Right Hon'ble Dr. Tej Bahadur Sapru paid a flying visit to Lahore. At a grand reception held in his honour by the Punjab Literary League, Sir Gokul Chand Narang, in welcoming the distinguished guest remarked that Sir Tej was one of those few eminent Indians who were at once trusted by the Government and respected by the Public. No doubt, the same can easily be said about Rai Bahadur Ram Saran Das without any modification. He has received great recognition at the hands of the present Government. After inheriting a seat in Durbars, he attended Lord Elgin's Durbar held in Lahore. He was a Government guest at Delhi Coronation Durbar as also at the Durbar held by H.R.H. the Prince of Wales at Lahore in 1905. He was also invited recently to attend the Coronation of their Majesties in London and was the guest of the British Government there. In 1906 he was nominated a member of the Committee of Management, Govt School of Engineering and of the Victoria Jubilee Institute in 1907. In 1905 the Government appointed him as Joint Secretary of the Kangra Valley Earthquake Relief Work, and he justified his appointment by rendering very valuable services to the helpless and the needy at much personal sacrifice. In 1906, the Rai Bahadur was exempted from the operations of the Indian Arms Act—a distinction which the Government bestows upon a few subjects. In 1933 he was the Northern India Chamber of Commerce delegate to the London Session of the Federated Chambers of the British Empire. He was also a Government delegate to the Reserve Bank Committee which met in London and in 1937 was a delegate to the Empire Parliamentary Conference held in London.

As regards his public life, he is equally popular with all communities. Many societies and organisations have honoured him with offices. He is President, Punjab Sanatan Dharma Pratinidhi Sabha, General President of the Sanatan Dharma College Managing Committee; President, All-India Khatri Sabha and being a big landlord himself is a prominent member of All-India Land Holders Association.

In the business wocietyof this province, his name is held in the highest esteem. He is Director, Imperial Bank of India; Chairman, Advisory Committee of the Central Bank of India Ltd.,(Punjab Branches); Chairman Indian Institute of Bankers (Pb. Branch); Vice-Chairman, British India Corporation Limited, Cawnpore; Director, The Indian Transcontinental Airways Ltd., Ex-Chairman, Northern India Chamber of Commerce; Vice-Chairman, Gwaliar State Economic Board of Development; Member, Punjab Government Development Board; Director, Sutlej Cotton Mills Co, Ltd., and last though not the least, Chairman of the Sunlight of India Insurance Co., Ltd., Lahore.

In U.P. he was given a civic address and was entertained by the Municipal Board of Cawnpore as well as of Lucknow. This goes to show his popularity in other provinces as well.

He has served on various Standing and Select Committees during the last 30 years in the Provincial as well as in the Central Legislatures.

The most outstanding thing about the Rai Bahadur is his religious bent of mind. Even from his boyhood he was fond of religious studies. Generally people turn to religious performances in order to better their material prospects or to overcome some difficulties and misfortunes. It is really a sight to see this multi-millionaire (who can equally command all the comforts and luxuries of life with the help of his great wealth) devoting each morning several hours to religious performances. Even his heavy business responsibilities and public engagements cannot stand in his way. He must always begin his daily programme after prayers. He is also a great student of various religions, and has studied thoroughly the sacred books of the Hindus. He says that he has also read with much devotion and profit the Holy books of the Muslims, the Sikhs and other religions. That appears to be the main cause of his non-communal tendencies. He has respect for all religions and hatred or prejudice for none. Sp people of all communities like his, equally.

During conversation with him, one can easily have an idea of his deep scholarship and wide learning in matters religious. It may be mentioned here that the Rai Bahadur appears to have no liking for books on poetry, drama, novel, fiction or short story, though he is a great admirer of Indian Music, Painting and ancient Architecture.

The Rai Bahadur is also a much travelled gentleman. He has travelled throughout India, Dutch East Indies, Jawa, Bali, Malaya, Siam, Indo-China. Burma, Ceylon, Egypt and has also visited every country in Europe, except Russia, Sweden, Denmark and Spain. It may be mentioned to his credit that throughout his wide travels in the East and West, he retained his usual Indian dress, which was greatly admired both at home and abroad. He says that sight-seeing is his hobby and that made him travel so much. During his visit to Europe he managed to go to the North Cape, saw the midnight sun, snow even on sea level, and the highest glacier of Europe. In one of the plays of Shakespeare, a character says, I have sold my lands to see others". Such, appears to be the case of the Rai Bahadur who must have undoubtedly spent a lot of money and time in travels which have in turn made him so rich in experience and thought.

Deep religious studies have made him thoughtful, sober and unemotional. He can sit for hours together in meditation. Yet he is very active and alert in his business and public life. In business he is accurate like a mathematician, and far sighted like British Traders. Even the minutest details, in home, office or factory receive his careful attention. Having imbibed the true spirit of religion, he would never injure the feelings of anybody. Even with his domestic servants, he behaved cordially and is loved and respected by them rather than feared as a master. He likes comforts, but hates luxuries and has a lively sense of humour. He is a great philanthropist and his charities exceed one million rupees which have been paid to various educational institutions, hospitals and other public bodies. He is very fond of children and finds delight in doing himself childish things before them.

ANNEXURE 2

TWO ARTICLES BY TAHIR KAMRAN ON MELA RAM AND RAM SARAN DAS PUBLISHED IN THE PAKISTAN, NEWSPAPER, THE NEWS ON FEBRUARY 19, 2017 AND FEBRUARY 26, 2017.

This was published 72 years after his death.

The face of modern Punjab—II
Tahir Kamran February 19, 2017
The contribution of Lala Mela Ram

Bengal Renaissance and the transformation that it entailed in the early 19th century is a theme of vital importance for the historians of South Asia. Permanent settlement of Bengal exhilarated the pace of transformation by undercutting the old order—with *zamindars* having unequivocal sway over the resources, both human as well as material. Introduction of the modern education system, new rules of governance and putting together a communication network were the key factors which played a permeating role in the re-invention of Bengal.

The emergence of *Bhadralok* (middle class or bourgeoisie) as a class was the most decisive outcome of the transition that occurred as a result of Bengal renaissance. Bhadralok, as shown by several scholars including Partha Chatterji, in the subsequent years, came to foment the sentiments of resistance against British imperialism. But more importantly that class became a conduit whereby Bengal was transposed from medieval to the modern epoch.

What I tend to argue in today's column is that a similar sort of transition took place in the Punjab after its annexation in 1849. Under John Lawrence and his successors, it underwent a period of thorough transition, opening up as a result, new spaces and opportunities for ambitious individuals and communities to prosper. Hindu Khatries were the main beneficiaries of the newly emergent situation. The era of modernity unleashed under the British brought Khatries as was the case of Bhadralok in Bengal, to the centre stage of socio-economic setting of the colonial Punjab.

The case of Mela Ram and his son Lala Ram Saran Das from Lahore is an illustration of that phenomenon of Punjabi bourgeoisie (you may read it Khatri too but Punjabi bourgeoisie by no means is restricted to Khatris) rising to prominence.

Lala Mela Ram was born in 1832 to Diwan Dhanpat Rai, a scion of a family which once was favourably poised during the days preceding Maharaja Ranjit Singh. Mela Ram's grandfather Diwan Das Mal flourished from 1747 to 1798 as a Commander of the Artillery under the Bhatties. The Zamzama, a historic cannon installed at the Mall Road, was then under his command. A person of multiple talents and valour, Diwan Das Mal achieved many distinctions which brought him great respect in the State. He died in 1798 when his only son Diwan Dhanpat Rai was only two.

The case of Mela Ram and his son Lala Ram Saran Das from Lahore is an illustration of that phenomenon of Punjabi bourgeoisie (you may read it Khatri too but Punjabi bourgeoisie by no means is restricted to Khatris) rising to prominence.

Shortly afterwards, Ranjit Singh marched on Lahore and established his rule over the Punjab. In the changes that followed, all the jagirs and properties of the Diwan family were confiscated and many of the family members were massacred. His maternal grandfather secretly took Dhanpat Rai away from Lahore to Batala, where he brought him up in obscurity and in relative poverty. Dhanpat Rai grew up in difficult circumstances. Mela Ram was born to him as a second son, Lala Ram Dyal being his eldest offspring. But the return of the fortunes and prestige of the family was mainly due to his younger son, Mela Ram, during whose life-time the Punjab passed from the domain of the Khalsa to that of the British.

Mela Ram demonstrated extraordinary courage and adaptability to take advantage of the changed situation which he turned to his favour.

Equipped with zeal and energy which he possessed in abundant measure, coupled with earnest desire to revive the old glories of his once magnificent family, Mela Ram got on with his practical life as contractor. By dint of hard work and integrity, he rose to the top of his profession. He took the entire contracts of Amritsar-Pathankot Railway, including iron-work, sleepers and masonry, which he finished within the stipulated time. That was no less than an extraordinary feat for which the government granted him a special reward of ₹50,000.

For the services he rendered, in February 1869, Mela Ram attained the distinction of being appointed a "Darbari" and seventeen years later was honoured with the title of "Rai Bahadur". Later on, he became an industrialist and set up the first textile mill in Lahore adjacent to Data Darbar, where several hundreds of people sought employment. Currently, that space is with Hizb-i-Ahnaf, and is probably under the legal ownership of Evacuee Trust Property Board (ETPB).

Like several other prominent people from Khatri caste i.e. Harkishen Lal, Ganga Ram, Mela Ram too had a charitable character. Besides, he lent financial support to various institutions along with helping poor sections of the society. He got a water tank built near the Railway Station and sunk many wells in different towns of the Punjab.

Such ventures like a hostel to feed the poor and a shop to provide flour to the destitute were really commendable. He generously donated large sums to the public sector institutions like Delhi Hospital (₹24,000 in 1864), Central Training College, Lahore (₹15,000 in 1886) and Lady Dufferin Hospital for Women (₹15,000 in 1886).

That is how these fellows left an enviable legacy. However, what distinguished Mela Ram and also his son Ram Saran Das was the social plurality which they demonstrated. Electrifying Data Darbar was one big illustration of their non-communal character. Then, at their house (Lal Haveli), all the occasions and festivals were celebrated with equal enthusiasm. Poetry symposiums (Mushairas) were held under their patronage at regular intervals.

Mela Ram is said to have donated 36 acres of land for the building of Lahore Zoo, which in itself was a great act of generosity. Lala Mela Ram died on April 10, 1890 leaving behind him two minor sons, the elder being Lala Ram Saran Das, who will be the topic of the next column because he was an important figure in his own right.

The face of modern Punjab III
Tahir Kamran February 26, 2017
The contribution of Lala Ram Saran Das

ShLala Ram Saran Das was born in Lahore Nov 26, 1876. He was just 14 when his father passed away and he came under the tutelage of his uncle. At that time he was studying in the

Central Model School.

After matriculating in 1897, he came to Government College Lahore and took the subjects of Science, Sanskrit and History. However, shortly afterwards his uncle too passed away forcing Ram Saran Das to shoulder the onerous responsibilities of managing his father's vast estates, contracts and *zamindari*. The obvious consequence was that Ram Saran Das had to quit his studies. But the adversity of circumstances could not deter him from taking full charge of his bequest which he managed admirably well. Inspite of being at a tender age, he gave a good account of himself by demonstrating maturity and not shirking from the hard work.

The first spinning and weaving mill in the entire province was the outcome of Lala Ram Saran Das's deep insight into business affairs and his skill and industry coupled with vast resources which his father had bequeathed to him. Sir Dennis Fitzpatrick, the then Lieutenant Governor of the Punjab formally inaugurated the mill in 1897. The remarkable aspect was Ram Saran Das' age; he was merely 21 when such a mega project came to fruition in which more than one thousand people found employment. He took extraordinary interest in all the spheres of its functioning and worked himself as a "Dispatcher, Correspondence-Clerk and Accountant."

He also gained practical experience as a mechanical and civil engineer which came in quite handy in administering the affairs of the mill in an efficient manner. His zeal as an industrial-business entrepreneur led him to expand his business concerns. He undertook large contracts for the construction of a Division of the Nagda-Mathura Railway where 12,000 people were employed. Various bridges, railway lines and magnificent buildings were built by his firm, Messrs. R. B. Mela Ram & Sons, Lahore.

Those were the days when Punjab's renaissance had reached its pinnacle point and the Khatri caste (Hindus) formed the pivot of the transformation that the province underwent during the last quarter of the 19th Century. Canal colonisation, initiated during the 1860s, had started bearing fruit by the close of the century, with the emergence of the rural bourgeois being an important outcome. The British administration got sensitised to the importance of the rural/ agricultural section, which was under distress because of the land alienation at the hands of money lenders who were also Khatris. Kirars, Auroras and Aggarwals were the main moneylenders.

It may be argued that since the British no longer bought cotton from America since the 1860s, they now needed to keep the Indian agricultural classes happy for business purposes.

It might seem inconceivable today that before British colonialism, there was no concept of private ownership of property in Punjab. With the arrival of the British, and with the advent of the capitalist ideas of private possession and a laissez faire economy, the Khatris, who had been businessmen for generations, were cognizant of the fact that an opportunity had presented itself. Since they had access to capital, and realised that the possession of land would entitle them to acquire social standing and influence in the Indian caste-based polity, they started buying agricultural and residential land in large areas.

What makes this process doubly interesting is that the Khatris were also moneylenders. As a result, many landowners would leave their land as collateral with the Khatri *banias* against the money they borrowed for everyday problems like birth, travel, marriage, and death. Since interest on the original borrowing kept compounding exponentially, eventually the original landowner was forced to forfeit his right to his land, and it would become the possession of the Khatri moneylender.

This rise of the Khatri businessmen as large landowners in Punjab, was noticed by the British administrators, particularly by S. S. Thorburn and Charlez Montgomery Rivaz, who came to the conclusion that the Khatris had become an exploitative class. It is interesting to note that the rise of the rural Khatri bourgeoisie in Punjab was actually a social transformation from their identity as a caste to a class, which was a radical development in the social history of India.

During Lord Curzon's tenure as Viceroy of India, the Land Alienation Act of 1901 was passed. This was a watershed moment because the British administrators through this Act divided land into agrarian and non-agrarian divisions, with some castes being classified in the former category, and others in the latter.

What this eventually resulted in was that the Khatris could not become landowners due to their political identity as the urban bourgeoisie. Their political interests were reflected in the anti-Imperial policies and identity of the All-India National Congress. It may be argued that since the British no longer bought cotton from America since the 1860s, they now needed to keep the Indian agricultural classes happy for business purposes as well. This collusion of political and business interests resulted in the eventual pressure on the British to arrest the rise of the Khatris. Once the Khatris' right to acquire rural land was forfeited, this resulted in a fall in their social status.

In these ostensibly adverse circumstances for the Khatris and the urban bourgeoisie, the sagacity of Lala Ram Saran Das was of great help to his survival. His business concerns not only remained intact, but socially and politically his influence kept soaring. At the age of 22, he was nominated as a member of the District Board of Lahore, an office he held for 20 years. For about 18 years, he also remained a municipal commissioner. In 1909, he was conferred with the title of Rai Bahadur. In 1914, he was awarded the Kaiser-e-Hind Gold Medal, and two years later, the CIE was conferred on him.

Under the Montford Reforms, he was elected to the Punjab Legislative Council. In 1930, his election to the Council of State came as a surprise to many. He was equally popular among the British and the Indians, and was respected across the colonial divide. In short, he was a member of numerous committees, did charity and relief work, and was influential in various circles.

The reason for his persistent popularity even in the times of the Khatris not being favoured by the British was that Rai Bahadur Ram Saran Das, despite his rise and wealth, never lost his innate humility, and maintained an educated and pluralistic outlook on life. His close friends were drawn from all social strata, regardless of class, wealth and religious association. His contribution for Punjab and specially Lahore was so immense that it can be said with conviction that upon his death in 1945, the glorious era of the rise of Punjabi bourgeoisie in colonial India lost one of its central figures.

(Concluded)

ANNEXURE 3

R.B. RAM SARAN DAS FAMILY TREE

SONS OF R.B. RAM SARAN DAS

1. R.B. GOPAL DAS was first married to Surajkanta. After her death he married Indumati.

He had eleven children.

(I) Chanderkanta married Parkash Chand Chopra. She had three sons and a daughter; Son-Pratima (deceased 2011) married Linda, daughter Nikola Paro: Son-Karan Prakash (deceased 2008), Son-Yadav Chopra married Jyoti, two sons-Dhruv and Uttam. Daughter-Shakti. **(II)** Nirmalkanta married Harbhajan Singh of Lucknow; two sons, Birendra and Himanshu (deceased). **(III)** Satyawan Jitendra, married Gool and had one son and daughter. All deceased except the daughter. **(IV)** Uma Kanta married Harbans Kapoor and had one son-now all deceased. **(V)** Shobha Maini had three sons and a daughter. Sons Naveen, Bharat, Bhushan and daughter Aarti. Living in Canada. **(VI)** Ripu Daman had two daughters. Sonia married Dr, Sachdeva, head of the ENT department, Max Hospital, Delhi. Chandini married Ajay Bahri working with Qatar Telecommunications as CFO in Doha. **(VII)** Inderjit childless divorcee, retired as a 747 (Jumbo) pilot from the airline Air-India and Air- Malayasia, settled in New Zealand.

(VIII) Indrani married to renowned agriculture scientist Anoop Singh Bedi, son of late Babaji Surinder Singh Bedi who sat on the 'Sikh Gaddi.' She has two daughters, Geetanjali and Nanki Shabnam. **(IX)** Indra Gopaldas Biel (now divorced). Retired as an international consultant and export manager for L'oreal, France. Lives in Paris. **(X)** Ravinder Chadha does farming in Karnal, Haryana. Has one son, Arvind (Capt. in Air- India), two daughters, Deepika (married to Gagan Katyal) settled in California and Dipti married to Shiveer Singh living in Chandigarh. **(XI)** Kaminder retired from Oracle as computer programmer, settled in Washington. U.S.A.

2. Wing Commander (Honorary rank given by Royal Indian Air Force) RUP CHAND

Married Vilas and had three sons. One died at an early age. **(I)** Elder son Suraj Bahadur(deceased) has two children. Uday, an entrepreneur, and Shobha married to Dalip Jolly, an entrepreneur. **(II)** Shakti (deceased) married to Sanjukta has two daughters and a son. Divya married Prakash Kunal, son Tiger Bahadur married Jyoti and a younger daughter Mimi Bahadur.

3. RAVI SHANKER

Ravi Shanker married Pushpa and had two sons.

(I) Sunil married Meera and had a daughter Shibani. **(II)** Nitin married Poonam and had two daughters, Gunjan and Parul.

4. JAGDISH CHANDER

Jagdish Chander married Primla. They had three daughters and a son.

(I) Nilima (known also as Nina) married Satinder Lambah former Special Envoy to the prime minister and Ambassador to Pakistan, Germany and Russia. They have two children, son Vikram and daughter Diya. **(II) & (III)** twin daughters Nikita and Babli. **(IV)** Son Deepak Chander married Nandita and has a daughter, Seher and son Jai).

5. RAJESHWAR BALI

Rajeshwar Bali married Primla (popularly called Gulu). They have a daughter and two sons.

(I) Anjali, married Raj Sawhney and had two sons, Viraj and Arjun, **(II)** Arvind married Reba and had a daughter Pooja and son Amar. **(III)** Pavan the youngest, deceased, married Vanita and had two sons Shaunak and Shauriya.

DAUGHTERS OF R.B. RAM SARAN DAS

R.B. Ramsaran Das had three daughters.

(I) The eldest **Gopal Dei** married Diwan Badrinath (prime minister of Jammu and Kashmir under the later Maharaja Hari Singh) and had two daughters. Sheila married Narinder Singh a barrister from Kanpur. She had 2 sons and 2 daughters. Bhirendra Jeet Singh married Namita, Virender Jeet Singh married Nandita, Kirti married Mehra and Kiran married Mehra **(II)** Padma married diplomat B.K. Kapoor, Secretary in the Ministry of External Affairs and also Ambassador to Sweden. They had a son Arun (deceased) married to Ritu.

2) **Lalita** married Shambu Lal Puri and had 11 children.

(I) Kanta Tandon married Dr. G.C. Tandon and had a daughter Meera who married Dr. B.M.L. Kapoor. (surgeon ex AIIMS. Now in Apollo Hospital). **(II)** Wing Commander Tapeshwar Puri married Kaushalaya and had 3 children. Aditya (married Anita) is, Managing Director HDFC. Adeshwar (married

Neeta) and they are into consulting and business events. Arti married Col. Sudhir Sood. **(III)** Rajender married O.C. Malhotra and had 3 children. Vinod (IAS) (married Nisha (IRS), Veena (married Vijay Chopra of the State Bank of India, and Vikram(married Preeti) is with ONGC. **(IV)** Sita married M.L. Kampani who was with the army, civil service and retired as Lt.Governor Andaman and Nicobar Islands. They had 3 children. Karan (married Sharda) who was with a tea company, Kiran is with Salwan Public school married Randhir Mehta who deals with trading commodities and Arjun (married Anila) also deals in international trading of commodities. **(V)** Uma married Lt.Gen V.C. Khanna and had 2 children. Uday (married Deepa) and was Chairman of Lasarge/Bata and earlier with Hindustan Lever; Renu married Paritosh Gulati who runs his own company (INWBIS). **(VI)** Usha married H.K.L. Capoor, IAS Chief Secretary Gujerat and Chairman UPSC and had 4 children. Deepa (married Uday), Ashok, ex-President U.B. Group married (Kalyani.). Indu, Director of the Institute Chetna in Ahmedabad married Debashish an architect and Jyoti who remained single is a writer. **(VII)** Tilak Puri married Sharda and had 2 children. Bharat Puri married Alka, Managing Director Cadbury and now Managing Director Pidilite. Shivani Chib, a teacher in Vasant Valley School married Col. Chib who is with Chowgules. **(VIII)** Sharda, who held cooking classes, married Ravi Thapar who was Chairman of Oriental Insurance. They have 2 children Rajiv, who has his own chartered accountant firm, married to an Australian, (Susan), who is a sports woman and an alpinist. Sanjay was with American Express in Singapore and now has his own consulting firm, married Poonam, a teacher. **(IX)** Munishwar Puri a lawyer married Pamela and they have 3 children. Meenakshi, a teacher in

D.P.S. Vasant Kunj, married to Rajan Dutt who works with Mohan Meakin. Anjali Puri works in HDFC. Urvishi, a teacher married to Alok Tandon M.D. Inox. Deepali married Sandip Sandhu, a businessman in Amritsar. **(X)** Rameshwar Puri, a lawyer married Saroj, a horticulturist. They have 2 children Shekhar(deceased) a lawyer. Shalini teaches in London and is married to Samir Kaushal who works for Standard Chartered. **(XI)** Saroj, a teacher in Sophia College, Bombay also does her own insurance business, married to Yograj Kakar a businessman in Bombay. They have 2 children. Sundeep MD City Bank married to Alka and Bobby married to Ritu, works with a bank in Dubai.

3) KANS, married B.K.Chopra and had 5 children, Vijaya, Pido who married Shanti, Ranjit, Gaggo(who died as a young boy) and Shruti married to Chander Pahwa of Allahabad.

FAMILY OF HARKISHEN DAS (younger brother of Ram Saran Das) died at the age of 29.

Harkishan Das had two daughters.

1. **Roop Kaur**, married R.B. Bashiram Sahgal and had 2 daughters and 2 sons **(I)** Bimla, married General Pran Nath Thapar, who became the 5th Army Chief of India. They had three daughters, Premila, Shobha, Kiran and a son Karan, who is the famed TV anchor. **(II)** Nirotam Sahgal, joined the ICS and had two sons, Arjun and Bharat. **(III)** Gautam Sahgal was the head of Ciba. (He married Nayantara – daughter of Vijay Lakshmi Pandit and niece of Jawahar Lal Nehru). He had two daughters, Nonika and Gita and a son Ranjit. **(IV)** Premilla married the son of V.P. Menon and had a daughter, Nalini and son, Lakshman.

2. **Mohan Kaur** married Vidya Dhar, had three children. **(I)** & **(II)** of whom, Kamla and Mahindra died young. **(III)** Savitri married Diwan Lai and has a son, Rabin who married Dolly, daughter of Darbari Seth of the Tata Group, a senior executive in ITC. Rabin has two children.

FAMILY OF LAXMI ANAND (SISTER OF R.B. RAM SARAN DAS)

She had four daughters. Family tree of only the youngest daughter available.

Puran Dei married Sahib Dayal Suri (Advocate) and had 5 sons and a daughter. Sons were Avinash Suri, Kailash Suri, Subhash Suri, Ramesh Suri and Kamlesh Suri. No further information available. Daughter Kiran married Maj Gen. S.K. Behl and had a son, Sanjay (partner Deloitte USA) married to Radhika and a daughter Radhika married to Dr. Sanjay Sobti.

ANNEXURE 4

ARBITRATION AWARD DISTRIBUTING PROPERTIES OF R.B. RAM SARAN DAS AFTER HIS DEATH

Reproduced below is arbitration award distributing the properties other than agriculture land of Rai Bahadur Ram Saran Das after his death in 1945. Given to the author by Ripudaman, son of R.B. Gopaldas-

ENGLISH CIVIL FORM No. 35.

DECREE IN SUITS FOR POSSESSION, & C.

(Order XX, rule 7, of the Code of Civil Procedure)

In the court of Mr. S.A.Nasir, B.A. Bar-at-law, Senior Sub Judge Lahore.

Case No 117 of 1946

Mr. Daya Kishen Mahajan, Advocate, Lahore.......Arbitrator

Vs.

1. RBL Gopal Das, 2. The Honble F/ Lt Rup Chand, 3. Mr. Ravi Shankar, 4. Mr. Jagdish Chander, 5. Mr. Rajeshwar Bali sons of Hon'ble R.B.L. Ran Saran Das, C.I.E. of 1, Edgerton Road, Lahore..............Respondents.

Petition under Section 14 (2) of the Indian Arbitration Act 1940 of the Arbitrator.

Plaint presented on the 26-7-46

Value of suit for purpose of jurisdiction ₹10000000/- .

This suit has come on this day for final disposal before me Mr. S.A. Nasir, B.A. Bar-in-law, Senior Sub Judge, Lahore in the presence of Mr. Rattan Lal Chawla, Advocate for the Arbitrator and R.B.L. Gopal Das in person Hon'ble Flight Liut. Rup Chand with Mr. Jinder Lal, Advocate, Mr. D.N. Avasthy, Advocate for Ravi Shankar; It is ordered that the award be filed and a decree be and the same id hereby passed in accordance with the terms of the award. (Copy attached herewith).

COSTS OF SUIT

	Petitioner		Respondents	
1.	Stamp of power	1/-/-	Stamp of power	5/-/-
2.	Do for power	-/-/-	Do for petition	2/-/-
3.	Do for exhibits	-/-/-	Pleader's fee on	₹-/-/-
4.	Pleader's fee on	₹-/-/-	Subsistence for witnesses	-/-/-
5.	Subsistence for witnesses	-/-/-	Service of process	-/-/-
6.	Commissioner's fee	- / - / -		
	Commissioner's fee	-/-/-		
7.	Service of process	1/-/-		
	Total	2/-/- not due	Total	7/-/- not due

Given under my hand and the seal of the court this, 27th day of August, 1946.

(Sealed)
Ram Saran Das
2-10-46

S/d. S. A. Nasir,
Senior Sub Judge Lahore

In the court of Mr. S. A. Nasir, B. A. Bar-at-law, Senior Sub Judge Lahore.

Case No.117

Plaint presented on the 28-07-46

Mr. Daya Kishan Mahajan Advocate, Lahore, Arbitrator.

Vs.

R. B. L. Gopal Dass, 2. The Hon'ble F/Lt Rup Chand 3. Mr. Ravi Shankar, 4. Mr. Jagdish Chander, and 5. Mr. Rajeshwar Bali sons of the Hon'ble R.B.L Ram Saran Dass, C.I.E. of 1, Egerton Road, Lahore ....Respondents.

Claim petition under Section 14(2) of the Indian Arbitration Act.

As differences arose amongst the parties above named owing to the constant ill health of the Hon'ble Rai B.L. Ram Saran Dass, C.I.E. the father of the parties and the karta of the Joint Hindu Family, running under the name and style of "R. B. Mela Ram's Sons" Lahore, under a registered agreement dated the 17th October, 1945, I was appointed an arbitrator to give an award on the following matters in difference between them :-

1. The management of Joint Hindu Family estate and its affairs.
2. The principles and mode of partition of the family properties and businesses and of their actual partition by metes and bounds.
3. The account ability of the members of the family Interse as regards the family estate.

The arbitrator agreement was signed by the Hon'ble R. B. L. Ram Saran Dass and by Shrimati Amrit Kaur (Mrs. Ram Saran Dass) who agreed to take maintenance to be fixed by me in lieu of her share on partition. The father had no objection to the partition being made among his sons.

I entered upon this reference on the 2nd of November

1945. The time for making of the award was extended by the Senior Subordinate Judge Lahore twice. The first extension of four months was granted on the 14th February 1946 and the second of one month on the 30th of May 1946. The award is being delivered within the time allowed by the Court. These extentions were necessitated by reason of the sad demise of the Hon'ble R. B. L. Ram Saran Dass on the 23rd of November 1945, the complicated nature of the questions involved, and of the extensive nature of the estate to be partitioned.

As regards the first matter in difference, it is not now necessary to give any award. The joint Hindu family estate and its affairs were managed by the parties themselves under my supervision and advice from the 2nd of November 1945 to the date of this award. All decisions taken in the matter of management are contained in the arbitration proceedings and need not be mentioned in the award. All that may be stated is that a part of the estate of the family was sold by the parties to meet its liabilities and to pay its debts. All debts known or discovered and claims received have been paid out of the current income and the sale proceeds of the property sold and no debt or liability except those mentioned in the award now remains due. However if any claim or liability still remains outstanding the parties will be jointly liable to pay it. If any asset or income has been omitted from consideration in the award the parties will be jointly entitled to it when discovered or realised. The parties now request me not to give any award on matters of management mentioned in para. No. 1 of the arbitration agreement as that para has exhausted itself and is no more operative.

As regards the difference mentioned in para No. 3 of the arbitration agreement the parties agree that no account of family estate need be gone into or rendered by any party. No award was therefore called on this point.

As regards the matter in difference in para No. 2 of the arbitration agreement, i may mention that most of them have been decided by me with the consent and concurrence of the parties and the decisions have been accepted by them. I now proceed to deliver my award on matters on which it is necessary to give an award:-

I. MAINTENANCE

a) I hereby direct the parties to invest out of the joint family estate a sum of ₹10,00,000/- (Rupees Ten Lakhs) with the Jupiter Investment Trust Ltd. In Fixed Deposit at a rate of interest to be fixed by the arbitrator and the parties in the joint names of the parties for the life time of Mrs. Ram Saran Dass. The interest of this amount is payable to her as maintenance in lieu of all her claims against or over the joint family property. After her death, the five sons of the late Hon'ble R. B. L. Ram Saran Dass (parties to this reference) their heirs, successor or assigns will be entitle to divide this amount equally along with any interest accuring due after the death of Mrs. Ram Saran Dass. This amount is not payable to the parties during her life time. The Fixed Deposit receipt shall be kept for safe custody with the Directors of the private limited company of the parties (i.e. R. B. Mela Ram's Sons).

b) I also direct that Mrs. Ram Saran Dass be provided for her life time with a suitable residence, joint or separate at her choice. This will be provided by her three sons, Mr. Ravi Shankar, Mr. Jagdish Chander, and Mr. Rajeshwar Bali. R.B.L. Gopal Dass or the Hon'ble F/Lt. Rup Chand, it is hereby declared, are not liable to provide any residence for her.

c) I further direct that Mrs. Hari Kishan Dass (Shrimati Dhanwant Kaur) be given a sum of ₹1200/- (Rupees one thousand & two hundred only) per mensum as maintenance allowance as agreed by the late Hon'ble R.B. L. Ram Saran Dass. She is living in a haveli in Kucha Rai Bahadur L. Mela Ram, Bhati Gate, Lahore (which is now valued at ₹30,000) in lieu of her right of residence, the joint Hindu family has been effecting repairs to this haveli and has been providing a chowkidar for it. About her rights, I declare the following arrangement for her life time:-
   i) The amount of ₹1200/- per mensem will be a charge on all the properties allotted to each co-parcener.
   ii) The parties will pay their respective share of the sum of ₹12000/- every month. To effectively discharge this liability, they have given guarantees of Banks names below:-

R. B. LALA GOPAL DASS. In the sum of ₹1200/- by the Co-operative Bank, Lahore.

THE HON'BLE F/Lt. RUP CHAND In the sum of ₹240/-
MR. RAVI SHANKAR

MR. JAGDISH CHANDER In the sum of ₹720/- of the
AND New Bank of India, Limited
Mr. RAJESHWAR BALI Lahore.

The guarantees are irrevocable in the life time of Shrimati Dhanwant Kaur and are entrusted for safe custody with the Directors of the private Limited concern above mentioned.

(i) Shrimati Dhanwant Kaur will remain in possession of

residential haveli till her life time and on her death, it will become partiable amongst the parties in five equal shares.

(ii) The Directors of the Limited concern above named shall be under a legal obligation to provide a chowkidar for the haveli and to effect necessary repairs to it.

(a) SHRIMATI GIANO DEVI is a cousin of the parties and was being maintained by the late Hon'ble R. B. L. Ram Saran Dass. In order to respect the old arrangement I hereby direct that a sum of ₹100/-(Rupees One Hundred only) per mensem be paid to her for her life time. The Liability to pay this amount will be of the limited concern of the parties, i.e. R. B. Mela Ram's Sons Limited.

Shrimati Giano Devi is residing in a part of a haveli, situated inside the city i.e. in Kucha Mela Ram. To whichever party this house is allotted at partition, the liability to provide residence for her will be on him.

II. CHARITABLE PROPERTIES.

(a) Certain properties, a list of which is annexed to this award and marked Ext. I, have been used for charitable purposes and have been dedicated to those purposes by the family. With the agreement of the parties, I declare that hencefor4th these will be managed in the capacity of the Trustees by the Directors, whoever they may be of the private limited concern. 'R. B. Mela Ram's Sons.'

(b) I direct that in order to commemorate the memory of the late Hon'ble R. B. L. Ram Saran Dass, a sum of ₹100000/- (Rupees One Lakh) be taken out of the joint family estate and be deposited in Fixed Deposit with the Jupiter Investment Trust Ltd. at 4% per annum. I have been authorised by the parties to donate it for building a block in the memory of the deceased in an Educational Institution to be selected by me with the consultation of the parties, preferably, in the proposed Engineering College, Lahore.

III. LIMITED CONCERN AND BUSINESSES

(a) During the life time of the Hon'ble R. B. L. Ram Saran Dass, a private limited company. "R. B. Mela Ram's Sons" was incorporated and the properties of the family i.e. the Mela Ram Cotton Mills and Lal Kothi were proposed to be transferred to the limited company for the object of the company. A deed of transfer was registered after his death and new directors were elected by the company. The shares in the company are held by the parties equally. These properties are therefore, left out of the partition and will remain in the ownership of the private limited company.

(b) As regards the business, the family was executing a few contracts, particularly of the manufacture and supply of tents to the Government. It was also running the business of manufacture of cloth and yarn, in the Mela Ram Cotton Mills. It was decided to close these businesses. The assests and the liabilities of the businesses were taken over by R. B. L. Gopal Dass, who deposited in the arbitrator's account the then value of the assests taken over with the consent and the concurrence of all the members of the family.

(c) The Mill and Lal Kothi were leased under a registered deed of lease by the parties and the private limited company to R. B. L. Gopal Dass at a rental of ₹12000/- per mensem, for a period of three years, beginning with the 1st of January, 1946. The arbitrator is, therefore, no longer called upon to give an award with regard to these businesses. The terms of the lease deed and the articles of the private limited company will govern the relations of the parties in future qua these matters.

IV. PROPERTIES EXCLUDED FROM PARTITION

These properties cannot be partitioned owing to their position and certain circumstances, but I hereby declare that each of the party when actually effect partition thereof shall pay proper stamp duty at the time of execution of regular deed. For convenience of management it was considered necessary by the parties with my concurrence to exclude the following family properties from partition and to keep them in joint management. This management will be entrusted to the private Ltd. concern.

(a) MOVEABLE NAMELY:-

i. Library books contained in list Ext. 2.
ii. Account books contained in list Ext. 3
iii. Title deeds mentioned in list Ext. 4
iv. Certain movable properties kept joint for ceremonial occasions and for purposes of loaning to various needy persons, contained in Ext. 5.
v. Furniture etc. in Lal Kothi contained in Ext. 6.
vi. Carriages and Cars mentioned in list Ext. 7.
vii. Articles in safe mentioned in Ext. 8.
viii. Shares and prize Bonds mentioned in list Ext.9.
ix. Dividends due on shares of the family upto the 30th of June 1946, contained in list Ext.10.
x. Certain outstandings and unrealised incomes

contained in list Ext. 11.

xi. Any balances that remain in the Arbitrator's account after making disbursements, Ext.12

xii. Any balances in any banks in the joint names of the family before 1st of July 1946 Ext.13.

IMMOVABLES NAMELY:-

i. A Haveli in possession of Shrimati Dhanwant Kaur.

ii. Three Marlas of land behind the Vetrinary College.

iii. Two plots of land, 15 feet wide in Mela Ram Park 1, Abbot Road, Lahore.

V. JOINT LIABILITIES

The following liabilities litigation, and claims etc are to be paid met or settled or fought by the limited company on behalf of the five brothers:-

i. Any deposit, securities etc. of the tenants or employees lying with the joint family before 1-7-46.

ii. Claim by the Income Tax Department.

iii. Liability to run kot Mela Ram School for nine months.

iv. Fighting out the case against Messrs Kirparam Chunilal and its consequences.

v. Litigation with Kailash Kapur Trading Company, and Messrs Sukhdial & Sons and its consequences.

vi. Any subsequent litigations or disputes that may arise on behalf of or against the family relating to the period prior to 1-7-46.

VI. PROPERTIES HELD NOT PARTIBLE

By agreement of the parties it is declared that jewellery ornaments, house hold effects and other effects of movable character in possession of either of the parties or the ladies of the family are not liable to partition. They are therefore, declared the absolute properties of those who were in possession of the same at the date of the partition.

Mrs. Ram Saran Dass is declared the absolute owner of the personal movable left by the Hon'ble R. B. L. Ram Saran Dass on his death.

VII. AGRICULTURAL LANDS.

The parties have privately partitioned the agricultural lands belonging to the family along with any constructions machineries etc. that were on those lands and were meant for agricultural purposes. The live-stock on those lands was also treated as part thereof and by agreement went with the lands. Parties have made applications to the revenue authorities to give effect to this private partition made by them. I was absolved by them from giving any award about agricultural lands and to declare their rights in those lands. This matter in difference between the parties contained in the agreement was excluded from the reference with my consent during the arbitration proceedings. Therefore I am not called upon to give any award in this matter.

VIII. DISPOSAL OF CERTAIN PROPERTIES.

To determine the total value of the partible properties of the joint Hindu family certain movable and immovables properties like fodder, food-grains, outstandings etc., and Ichhra lands were given and taken at an agreed valuation by different parties amongst themselves. They deposited the amounts due in the arbitrator's account. The properties contained in list Ex. 14 are declared as properties of those parties against whose names they are mentioned in the list.

IX. PROVISION FOR RAJESHWAR'S MARRIAGE.

To mutual agreement, a sum of ₹65,000/- was set apart from the joint family estate for the marriage expenses of Mr. Rajeshwar Bali, the only unmarried coparcener of the family. This amount has been deposited with the New Bank of India Ltd. in a fixed deposit and will be payable to him by the Bank under instructions from the arbitrator when he is satisfied that Mr. Rajeshwar Bali is going to get marriage.

X. PARTIBLE PROPERTIES AND INDIA PARTITION.

The partible moveable and immovable properties were determined by me to be of the value of Rupees One Crore. The share of each party therefore came to Rupees twenty lakhs. Separate lists of properties of equal value were drawn up and were accepted by the parties as correct. Lots were then drawn with the result that the properties noted as under against each party fell to his share. Necessary adjustments in value were made between the parties by cash payment.

R. B. L. GOPAL DASS

(a) LAHORE PROPERTIES.

1. 4 Race Course Road, Lahore (S. 42 R I) area 72 Kanals 19 marlas and 55 feet.
2. Bungalows No.17,19 and 21 Abbot Road, with tennis lawns (SE 26R 30) (SE 26R 34), (SE 26R 36) and (SE 26R 38).
3. Lahore City House, A.417, B.560, B-1306, A.2118, A. 1378, A. 1377, A. 2120

(b) LYALLPUR PROPERTY

Clock Tower Shops & Ihata, Khasra No.3042/43.

(c) KANGRA PROPERTY

Gopal Bagh, Ghurkari (Kangra)

(d) CASH ₹15,000/- (Rupees Fifteen thousand only)

(e) SHARES

3000 shares of the Indian National Airways Ltd. Delhi (500 out of which are deferred shares) 100 shares of the Hindustan Commerical Bank Ltd. 35 shares of Reserve Bank of India

XI LIEUT. RUP CHAND

(a) LAHORE PROPERTY

Bungalow No.68 The Mall, Lahore (SR19R89) area 64 kanals 11 marlas and 103 feet.

Bungalow No.47 Lower Mall (SW93R46) are 14 kanals, 1 marla and 10 feet.

Lahore City hosues:- B-603, B-561, B-578, B-579.

(b) LYALLPORE PROPERTY

Rail Bazar shops and houses and shops in Mandi Khasra No.3604/5 and 3608/9.

(c) AMRITSAR PROPERTY

1. Bungalow No.114 on the Mall, area 24 Kanals.
2. Bungalow No.9, Amritsar Cantt.
3. Tawela and Baithak in Katra Kanahyan, No.1116 & 1117.
4. Haveli in Katra Jaimal Singh No.1469.
5. Shops in Bazar Pashamwala No. 1487,1488,1499,1500 and 1501.
6. House in Katra Dulo, No.3811/10.

(d) Bungalow "Alvely" Bakrota Hill, Dalhousie

(e) Cash: ₹12890/- (Rupees twelve thousand eight hundred and ninety only)

(f) Shares:-

British India Corporation-5600 ordinary, 50 Mining and Chemical Industries-1000 preferential. U.P.

Electric Supply Coy, 200 ordinary Northern Bank of India-10 Attock Oil Company, -500.

MR. RAVI SHANKAR : -

(a) LAHORE PROPERTY.

Bungalow No.4,14,15 and 16 Abbot Road (SE26R11, SE26R19, SE26R21, SE14R34) area 163 Kanals, 6 Marlas and 82 feet.

Lahore City Houses:—A-597, A-598, A-394, A-395, A-494, A-46, A-1758, A-1394, C-3874.

(b) LYALLPUR PROPERTY

Gol Bazar Shops and houses, Khasra Nos.333349/50 and 3345/46.

(c) DHARMSHALA PROERTY.

"Swarg Ashram" Site known as 'Folly'

Motor Garrage and open land annexed to Swarg Ashram

(d) CASH:-₹4760/-(Rupees Four thousand seven hundred and sixty only)

(e) SHARES:-

Central Bank of India	...	608
O. K. Electric Company	...	500
Premier Automobiles	...	1000
U. P. Western Electric	...	200
Northern Bank of India Rawalpindi	...	10

MR. JAGDISH CHANDER

(a) LAHORE PROPERTY

Bungalow No.1 Egerton Road Lahore (SE27R11) area 47 Kanals 18 marlas and 55 feet.

Bungalows no.2 & 4 Kashmir Road and adjoining open land (SE35 R6 and SE35 R4) area 83 kanals, 19 marlas and 165 feets.

Bungalow no.51 Lower Mall (SE93 R50) area 19 kanals 13 marlas and 140 feets.

City houses no.A2095, A2080, A2081

(b) LYALLPUR PROPERTY.

Jhang Bazar shops and Ihata, Khasra No.4350.

(c) Muree Hills "Belle Vue" on Kashmir point.

(d) Cash ₹9850/- (₹Nine thousand eight hundred and fifty only)

SHARES

Attock Oil Company Ltd. 676

Associated cements Ltd. 85

Hindustan Motors 100

Concord of India Insurance Coy 500

Lahore Electric supply Coy. Ltd. 14 and 140 (B. Class)

New India Insurance Company Ltd. 50

Mining Company Limited Simla 1000

Ambala Electric Supply Coy. Ltd. 25

MR. RAJESHWAR BALI

(a) LAHORE PROPERTY

Bungalow No.4 Egerton Raod, Lahore, (Se27R12) with adjoining open land, area 85 Kanals 18 marlas and 193 feet. Bungalow No.9 Cooper Road, (Se 34R 16) are 24 Kanals, 15 marlas, and 142 feet.

Bungalow No.31 Lower Mall (SW93 R 36) area 11 Kanals, 8 marlas and 153 feet.

Montgomery Road open land 13 Kanals and 213 feet.

Hari Kishan Dass Theatre (SW 38R 251)

New Ihata (Opposite Muslim High School)

Sillah Khana on Mela Ram Road, (Opposite Meleram Cotton Mills (SW 92R 7) area 3 Kanals 15 marlas, 29 feet.

Plot on mele Ram Rad, on the back of Wellington Talkies Khasra No.80 min. Area 11 marlas and 104 feet.

Open land near Data Ganj Baksh area 5 Kanals 2 marlas and 15 feet.

City Houses. A561, A563, A564, A566, A567, A573, A574, A604, A580, A582, A585, A586, A587, A588, A1376, A2111, A2112.

(b) LYALLPUR PROPERTY

Shops and houses in Chauk Pindi Dass, Khasra No.3622/23, shops and Ihata in Gol Bazar between Karkhana and Jhang Bazar, Khasra No.3869/79.

Sangla Hill shops, Khasra No.112

(c) Shahpur Kandi Bungalow in the four wall of the Fort Khasra no.37 and Mauza Treti.

(d) Cash ₹117330/- (One lakh, seventeen thousand three hundred and thirty only)

(e) SHARES

Sutlej Cotton Mills Okara 1000
Sunlight of India Insurance Coy 200
Bharat fire and General Insurance Coy 250
Punjab National Bank Ltd. 4
Investors trust 700
Western U. P. Electric Supply Coy......................100
Northern Bank of Rawalpindi 15

Note:- The details and boundaries of the properties are full described in the lists attached

I award the above properties to the parties as mentioned aforesaid and declare that these are their separate properties, and that the other co-parceners will have no concern or connection with them. These are declared as separately owned by them with effect from the 1st of July 1946 and from that date they are entitled to their possession and income as separate owners.

XI. "MANORMA" I EGERTON ROAD, LAHORE

This house has been the family's residential house for sometime. It falls to the share of Mr. Jagdish Chander. He will however, be not entitled to reject the following members of the family, who can reside their till the 30th June 1948. He will be entitled to rent from them as follows if they continued in possession of the respective occomodation with them at the time.

R. B. L. Gopal Dass ....₹ 400/- P.M.
Hon'ble F/Lt. Rup Chand ....₹ 500/- P.M.
Mr. Ravi Shankar ....₹ 150/- P.M.
Mr. Rajeshwar Bali ....₹ 150/- P.M.

In case of default of payment of rent, he will be entitled to eject the defaulter or defaulters. They are however, at liberty to vacate whenever they like even before the 30th of June, 1948. The possession of the parties as at present of the houses, garage out-houses etc. , annexed to this house, will be maintained.

Lahore — Sd/- Daya Kishan Mahajan
Dated 17-07-46 — ARBITRATOR

ACKNOWLEDGEMENTS

There are many people, both family and friends, who have made this book possible.

I would like to thank my family members who provided information. The late Suraj Bahadur had initially suggested I write a book on my grandfather, my uncle Rajeshwar Bali,for providing glimpses of their life in Lahore; my cousins Shobha Maini settled in Canada, and Inderjit in New Zealand, for sharing recollections of their childhood and my cousin, the late Ripu Daman, for giving me the order of settlement reproduced in the annexure. Sunil Khatri for presenting me thirty years ago with the copy of the book, 'Punjab's Eminent Hindus, published by New Book Society; Lakshman Menon for sending me an article on grandfather, and my nephew Viraj Sawhney for circulating to the family the same article, on the occasion of my uncle, Rajeshwar Bali's 90th birthday. This encouraged me to do further research on my grandfather.

I deeply appreciate the help from Karan Thapar, Arjun Kampani and Yadav Chopra for providing information on the Family Tree; Ratan Lal Malhotra for sharing information on R.B. Ram Saran Das being one of the initial Foundation Donors to the Doon School from the Memorandum of the Doon School; Sarthak Dhawan for helping to put together all the photographs for the book and Neeraj Kodesiya for his encouragement.

My gratitude to the former Secretary General of the Rajya Sabha, Shumsher Sherif and Mr. Tikku for their help in getting the proceedings of the Council of State, pertaining to R.B. Ram Saran Das. Also thanks to the Nehru Museum Library for enabling me to get newspaper records from their archives.

Syed Babar Ali, founder of Lums University in Lahore, Pakistan, has been extremely helpful in providing valuable information regarding my family and grandfather. He is amongst those few today, who as a young boy knew my grandfather. The families had close ties and in addition, he had studied in school with my older cousins. Thanks to Professor Tahir Kamran of Lahore who researched useful data on my grandfather as a member of the Punjab Legislative Council. He also granted permission to reproduce two of his articles written in 2017 in 'The News', a leading Pakistani newspaper. One on my great grandfather Rai Bahadur Mela Ram and my grandfather Rai Bahadur Ram Saran Das, a hundred and twenty seven years after the death of the former and seventy two years after the death of the latter.

Even at a time when I had no plans to write this book, during my husband's first posting in Pakistan (1978-82), I recall some Pakistani friends being articulate about the family. Amongst them were Mr. G Moinuddin, ICS and two leading lawyers, Mr. M.A. Rehman and Mr. Batalvi. The latter two took us on a conducted tour of Lahore to see places connected with my family, including the Mela Ram Road, named after my great grandfather. Mr. A Rahim sent me an article by Hakim Ahmed Shuja, a former secretary general of the United Punjab Legislative Assembly who wrote on my great grandfather and grandfather. Another person who shared some interesting information was the late Pran Seth.

It was kind of Nandini Mehta to go through the manuscript and make useful suggestions.

I was fortunate that Shri K. Natwar Singh, author and

former minister for External Affairs, meticulously read the entire manuscript and made changes, bringing the book to its present form.

I am extremely grateful to Rupa Publications for efficiently and promptly publishing the book and making it a reality.

Lastly, but above all, I would like to thank my husband Satinder Kumar Lambah, my son Vikram and my daughter Diya for their unstinting support.

The research on my grandfather has been, at every step, a revelation for me. His verve for life and his many achievements have filled me with pride. As a proud granddaughter I am glad I set upon the task of writing about him, no matter how late. To keep his memory alive is the very least I can do for a grandfather I did not know, as he died before I was born.

With each successive generation and an ever expanding family it is so easy to lose sight of one's own. If nothing else I hope this will help future generations to re-connect.

New Delhi

June, 2020
Nilima Lambah